CANONICAL

AND

UNCANONICAL GOSPELS

With a Translation of the Recently Discovered Fragment of the
Gospel of Peter, and a Selection from the Sayings of Our
Lord not found in the Four Gospels.

BY

Wr Er BARNES, B.D.

FELLOW OF PETERHOUSE, AND THEOLOGICAL LECTURER AT
CLARE COLLEGE, CAMBRIDGE

LONDON

LONGMANS, GREEN, & CO.

AND NEW YORK: 15 EAST 16th STREET

1893

CANONICAL

AND

UNCANONICAL GOSPELS

a

TO

S. E. B.   F. W. B.

"For all live to Him."

b

PREFACE

MY object in writing the following pages is to throw light on a subject on which many important misconceptions prevail. Even educated people are content to speak as if the Four Gospels had no history at all, or as if they first appeared in the fourth century A.C., coming from an unknown source. This treatise, therefore, will not be wholly useless if it makes it clear that the Canonical Gospels were beyond all doubt received as The Four Authoritative Gospels at least one hundred and twenty years before Constantine established Christianity as the State religion. Neither the first Christian emperor (311–337 A.D.), nor the great Council of Nicæa (325 A.D.), had anything to do with " selecting," as some have supposed, our Four out of a large number of Gospels. If our Gospels were ever " selected " (and did not rather hold a position of authority from the first), the selection took place apart from the worldly influence of a half-pagan emperor, and certainly more than a century before his reign. In the time of Constantine, our Gospels had already a long and honourable history behind them.

But I do not write these pages simply to disprove the notion that the Gospels first became authorities in the fourth century A.C. Still more prevalent is the more plausible contention that the Four Gospels (with the exception of S. Luke) are not to be traced during the hundred and fifty years which immediately followed Our Lord's death. One object of this book is to show that this contention is false, and that even if it were true, it would be misleading. The main features of the Story of Christ's Life can be traced back continuously to within thirty years of His death. The *narrative* cannot be shaken, even if the usual authorities for it be proved to be more recent than we believe.

The argument might have been much strengthened by a statement of the evidence to be derived from the use of one or all of our Four Gospels by the chief schools of heretics of the second century. Even the author of "Supernatural Religion" admits that the evidence to be derived from Marcion's Gospel proves the existence of our Gospel of S. Luke as early as 140 A.D. But this evidence, together with other evidence drawn from the practice of heretical schools, is not given here, because it consists chiefly of a mass of linguistic detail. It may, however, be mentioned that all schools of Christian Gnostics of the second century, the Ophites, the Basilideans and the Eastern and Western schools of the Valentinians all alike appealed to our Gospel of S. John.

On the other hand, I have been careful to notice any evidence recently brought to light. Such evidence will be found chiefly under "Tatian" and "Hermas." I have also tried to impart some freshness to the treatment of the subject by drawing from the original authorities wherever it was possible. This is especially the case with Eusebius, Justin, and Tatian.

The *rôle* of an Apologist is an unpopular one, for it is supposed to be incompatible with a genuine search for truth. I confess that I am not dispassionate; I am not indifferent which way the controversy is decided. I rejoice that I am led to the conclusion that the evidence for the authority of our Gospels is not weak but strong. Yet such a temper can well coexist with a resolution to learn the truth. A complete Apologist has to apologize to himself as well as to his fellow-men; what is meat for them is meat for him; husks for them are husks for him too.

W. E. B.

CAMBRIDGE,
February, 1893.

CONTENTS

CONTENTS.

CHAPTER I.

WHY DO WE ACCEPT OUR FOUR GOSPELS?

The question to be answered: Were our Four Gospels received
by the Christian Church in the earliest times of which we
have information?—The second century our chief field of
inquiry—A sketch of the history of the second century—
Consolidation—Persecution—Apology—Heresy.

THE question before us is not as to the *inspira-
tion* of the Gospels. We are not going to try
to show that they are the very Word of God.
We believe that the Gospels were written under
the over-ruling providence of God, but this belief springs from the Christian consciousness,
and is not subject to proof. A Christian cannot
help believing that the Gospels are in some true
sense inspired, a non-Christian can hardly help
believing the opposite. There is no room for
argument here.

The case is different with regard to the question of the *canonicity* of the Gospels. The

question concerns now a matter of fact, and
therefore of evidence. Do we possess the same
authoritative documents of the faith as the
earliest Christians possessed ? Do we regard
as authorities for the story of Christ the
writings which they regarded as such authorities ? When we have our answer, we are very
near to the answer to the supreme question of
Christian evidences, *i.e.* Have we the same story
of the life and teaching and death of Christ as
the earliest Christians had ?

As soon as we are assured that we have the
very story in attestation of which the first
followers of Christ suffered or laid down their
lives, we already have good reason for belief,
but the story admits further testing. When
we try the Four Gospels by the ordinary tests
used to try the trustworthiness of any ancient
record, we are brought to the conclusion that
they contain the evidence of those who were
at once eye-witnesses and men of candour. It
is difficult to resist the conclusion that the
evangelists either had themselves moved among
the events of which they wrote, or else had
received their narratives directly from those
who had done so.

But, deeply important as this line of evidence is, it is not the one worked out in this little book. Internal evidence is best studied when the external credentials of the books in question have been carefully considered. The main purpose of this treatise is to sketch the evidence from which we conclude that the Four Gospels have been accepted from the earliest times as the authoritative accounts of the life, teaching, and death of the Lord Jesus.

If a new work of an old author, say a new play of Shakspere, were discovered now, its genuineness would of course be debated partly on internal grounds. Its style would be compared with the style of the acknowledged plays, and the allusions in it, historical, or antiquarian, or geographical, would be compared with the known state of things in the poet's day. It might conceivably stand these tests so well, that those best fitted to judge would feel morally certain of its genuineness. But the only thing which could place it above suspicion would be a knowledge of its history. Is it to be found in any really old edition of his plays? Is its title given in any old list of his works? Did any old writer ever quote from it as Shakspere's?

Questions of a similar kind arise about the Four Gospels. We propose to sketch their history, as far as it is known at present.

It is fortunately not necessary to give the whole history. From the beginning of the third century, the Church certainly treasured the Four Gospels as the primary documents of the faith. There is no room for dispute here. From this time, the Christian Fathers' writings are numerous and well preserved in the main, and by their numerous quotations leave no room to doubt that the Four Gospels were regarded as the kernel of Christian belief and teachings..

With the second century, the case is somewhat different. Of the Christian literature of that century hardly a tithe has survived. Much of what does remain was addressed to heathens, to whom it was of little use to quote Scripture. Thus, to some writers on the Canon, the second century has appeared an impassable gulf, to others a shallow stream which may be crossed by safe stepping-stones, if not by an easy bridge. A sketch of the history of the Church generally during the second century will be helpful, before touching on the history of the Gospels during the same period.

The second century was a time of (1) consolidation, (2) persecution, (3) apology, and (4) heresy.

1. It was a period of *consolidation*, for at the middle, or towards the end of it, the Mediterranean was girdled with a chain of Christian strongholds organized under bishops, and lending mutual support and counsel. Vigorous Christian Churches existed at Alexandria in Egypt, Antioch in Syria, Ephesus and Smyrna in Asia Minor, Athens and Corinth in Greece, at Rome, at Lyons in the South of France, at Carthage in North-western Africa. Communication between these congregations, both by letter and by travel, was active. Already Rome had given signs of becoming the centre towards which all other Churches turned.

2. The second century was also a period of *persecution*. The great Emperor Trajan set the example. There was an earthquake at Antioch about the year 115, during the emperor's stay there. The populace rose and said that the gods had sent it because of the Christians. But the Christians were strong at Antioch. A great tumult seemed imminent. Trajan, as a statesman and a soldier, would doubtless have pre-

ferred to leave religion alone, but a disturbance at Antioch, on the great road to the East, would have been as inconvenient to him as a riot in Trafalgar Square to an English ministry. It was expedient that one man should suffer for the people, and so Ignatius, the Bishop of Antioch, was sent to Rome to be tried or executed where his presence would not embarrass statesmen.

From the year 138 to 181 A.D. was the age of the Antonines, Pius and his adopted son, Marcus Aurelius. Gibbon has called this perhaps the happiest period in the history of mankind. It might have been so, but the virtues of the emperors did not avert persecutions from the Christians. At Smyrna, Polycarp, the disciple of S. John, was burned to death at the age of eighty-six, under the Emperor, whose surname was " The Pious," and the Churches of the South of France weltered in blood under the Emperor who was called " The Philosopher." Perhaps neither emperor was directly at fault; but the pity of it ! The century closed with a savage persecution at Carthage, and the beginning of one at Alexandria.

THE SCILLITAN MARTYRS.

To this period belongs the trial of the Scillitan martyrs, which took place at Carthage some time between 180 and 200 A.D. The written report of this trial has been known at least since the beginning of the seventeenth century; but Professor Armitage Robinson has recently published in the Cambridge "Texts and Studies" a form of the report shorter than any previously known, and probably preserving the actual shorthand notes taken at the trial.

The document so well illustrates the *wooden* rather than *cruel* attitude of Rome towards Christianity, that it is worth while giving it here. Leaving out a few merely formal phrases, for the sake of brevity, it runs thus :—

"In the year in which Præsens and Claudian were consuls, Præsens for the second time, on the 17th day of July, at Carthage, Speratus, Nartzalus, and Cittinus (three men), Donata, Secunda, and Vestia (three women), were brought into the council chamber; whereupon Saturninus, the proconsul, addressed them in these words : Ye can earn the pardon of our Lord the Emperor, if ye become again well disposed.

"SPERATUS. We have never done ill; we have not practised injustice; we have never spoken ill, but even when ill-treated, we have given thanks; because we obey Our King.

"SATURNINUS. We, too, are religious, and our religion is plain and simple; we swear by the genius of our Lord the Emperor, and pray for his preservation, as ye also ought to do.

"SPERATUS. If you will give me an undisturbed hearing, I will tell you the very Mystery of Simplicity.

"SATURNINUS. If you begin to speak evil of our rites, I will not listen. Spare yourself, rather, and swear by the genius of our Lord the Emperor.

"SPERATUS. *I* do not acknowledge the kingdom of this world; on the contrary, I serve that God whom no man has seen, nor can see, with these eyes. I have committed no theft; rather, I pay the required duty on anything I buy (N.B. The foregoing words are obscure), because I acknowledge my Lord, the King of kings, and Ruler of all nations.

"SATURNINUS (*to the other Christians*). Give up these opinions.

SPERATUS. Evil are the opinions of our

ん

heathen adversaries who slay men and utter false witness. (We paraphrase the rather obscure original.)

"SATURNINUS (*again to the other Christians*). Have no share in this folly!

"CITTINUS. We have none other to fear save the Lord our God, who is in heaven.

"DONATA. Honour to Cæsar as to Cæsar; but fear to God!

"VESTIA. I am a Christian.

"SECUNDA. That which I am I wish to remain.

"SATURNINUS *to* SPERATUS. Do you persist in the profession of Christianity?

"SPERATUS answered: I am a Christian, and with him all agreed.

"SATURNINUS. Do you wish for time to deliberate?

"SPERATUS. In so clear a case of right, there is no room for deliberation.

"SATURNINUS. What have you in your safe?

"SPERATUS. Books, and the Epistles of Paul, a righteous man.

"SATURNINUS. Accept a remand for thirty days, and reflect.

"SPERATUS answered again : I am a Christian, and with him all agreed.

"SATURNINUS, the proconsul, read the sentence from his tablet : The court finds that Speratus (and his companions) have confessed that they live according to the Christian religion ; and that they have obstinately refused to accept the opportunity offered them of returning to the customs of the Romans ; the penalty to be De- capitation.

"SPERATUS said : We give thanks to God.

"NARTZALUS. To-day we are martyrs in heaven ; we thank God.

"SATURNINUS, the proconsul, ordered procla- mation to be made by a herald as follows : I have ordered Speratus, and (eleven names follow) to be taken away to execution.

"ALL said : We thank God.

"And so all were crowned with martyrdom at one time, and they reign with the Father, and the Son, and the Holy Ghost, through all ages of ages. Amen." (See Professor J. A. Robinson, S. Perpetua, pp. 112–116.)

In the foregoing report, there is one sentence which has a bearing on the Canon of the New Testament, which is not unlikely to be misunderstood. The martyrs answer that their church-chest contains Epistles of Paul, and other books not named. It might be hastily concluded either that they did not possess our Gospels, or that they rated the Epistles more highly. But, surely, it is unsafe to conclude, from these words, anything more than that the martyrs possessed Epistles of S. Paul. A reasonable explanation exists why these should be specially mentioned. The Christians seemed to the Roman Government to be an International secret society, and their correspondence by letter would naturally awaken suspicion. The Christians themselves, on the other hand, were ready enough to produce S. Paul's letters in order to show how he enjoined submission to the higher powers.

3. But the second century was also a time of *Christian apology*, for wherever Christianity was assailed with the sword, it was defended with the pen. At Athens, Aristides, a Christian philosopher, presented an Apology to Hadrian, the one emperor who, from his curiosity in religious matters, is likely to have looked at such a document.

THE APOLOGY OF ARISTIDES.

Of this Apology it will not be amiss to say a word. It is interesting on three grounds: (1) because it is the earliest defence of Christianity extant; (2) because it is the type according to which several later Apologies were in great measure composed; (3) because, after being lost for centuries, it was discovered as recently as 1889.

Mr. Rendel Harris (now University Reader in Palæography at Cambridge), while on a visit to the Convent of S. Catharine on Mount Sinai, was shown a Syriac manuscript which had escaped the indefatigable inquiries of Tischendorf. Among its contents Mr. Rendel Harris discovered the long-lost Apology, which up to that day had been known to us only from a notice by Eusebius, the great Church historian, and from a few fragments of doubtful genuineness. The work is worthy of the age to which it belongs. It is not a piece of profound reasoning, but an utterance of deep conviction. It begins with a few words of lofty simplicity on the nature of the One God; it goes on to point out the errors of " barbarians," who worshipped Nature in different forms, of Greeks who worshipped gods

resembling men in weakness and vice, and of
Jews who worshipped One God, and did many
things acceptable to Him, but whose ceremonial
service was paid rather to angels than to God;
it next describes the blameless life of the Christians; finally, it calls upon all who know not
God to receive " incorruptible words," and so "an-
ticipate the dread judgment which is to come by
Jesus the Messiah upon the whole race of men."

Aristides' account of the Christian Faith is
worth repeating. (It will be noticed that he
speaks objectively as from the outside, and does
not give it as just his own confession. He speaks
of the Christian life also from the same outside
standpoint.) He writes—

" The Christians then reckon the beginning of
their religion from Jesus Christ, who is named
the Son of God Most High; and it is said " (*i.e.*
among the Christians) " that God came down
from heaven, and from a Hebrew virgin took
and clad Himself with flesh, and in a daughter
of men there dwelt the Son of God. This is
taught from that Gospel which a little while
ago was spoken among them as being preached;
wherein, if ye also will read, ye will comprehend
the power that is upon it. This Jesus, then, was

born of the tribe of the Hebrews; and He had
twelve disciples in order that a certain dispen-
sation of His might be fulfilled. He was pierced
by the Jews; and He died and was buried; and
they (the Christians) say that after three days
He rose and ascended to heaven; and then these
twelve disciples went forth into the known
parts of the world, and taught concerning His
greatness with all humility and sobriety."

Some points of the Apologist's description of
the life of the Christians are also too interesting
to omit. A few extracts must be given in this
place.

"The Christians, O King, are nearer to the
truth and to exact knowledge than the rest of
the peoples. For they know and believe in God,
. . . those who grieve them they comfort, and
make them their friends . . . their wives, O
King, are pure as virgins, and their daughters
modest . . . as for their servants or handmaids,
they persuade them to become Christians for the
love that they have towards them; and when
they have become so, they call them without
distinction brethren . . . if they hear that any
of their number is imprisoned or oppressed for
the name of their Messiah, all of them provide

for his needs, and if it is possible that he may be delivered, they deliver him. And if there is among them a man that is poor and needy, and they have not an abundance of necessaries, they fast two or three days that they may supply the needy with their necessary food . . . if any righteous person of their number passes away from the world, they rejoice and give thanks to God, and they follow his body, as if he were moving from one place to another . . . And truly this people is a new people, and there is something divine mingled with it." (Rendel Harris, " Apology of Aristides," pp. 36–51.)

Such was the appeal of the Church to the Empire during the reign of Hadrian (117–138 A.D.)

At Rome, a few years later, Justin Martyr of Samaria addressed his defence of Christianity to Antoninus Pius and the Senate of Rome. I do not know what effect it had, but he seems to have been put to death shortly after. Lastly, just at the close of the century, Clement of Alexandria, and Tertullian of Carthage, wrote Apologies, the one sweet, reasonable, and philosophic; the other defiantly Christian. If Tertullian sounds too bitter now, as we read him in

our armchairs, it is well to remember that op-
pression drives even wise men mad.   And Tertullian, though great, was hardly wise.   Eloquent,
illogical, fiercely right and splendidly wrong, he
is one of a type of men not yet extinct, whose
hearts are greater than their heads.

4. The second century was also the century
of *heresy*, especially of Gnosticism.   The Gnostics
were to the Church its greatest evil and its
greatest good.   The majority of them might be
described as bankrupt philosophers, who re-
floated their philosophy on Christian credit.
Such men were philosophers first and Christians
only in the second place; but the fact that they
used the Name of Christ at all is a significant
proof that heathenism was dying.   They en-
grafted on the living tree of Christianity shoots
cut from the dying trunk of heathenism.

The heathen had for centuries been occupied
with speculations with regard to the origin of
the world through evolution of some kind.
These speculations the Gnostics carried on, and
thought to find in them an explanation not only
of the physical universe, but also of Christianity
and of moral evil.   This ancient theory of evolution differed from similar modern theories by

the slenderness of the evidence alleged for it, by
the poetical rather than scientific form in which
it was expressed, and, above all, by the fact that
it embraced the unseen universe no less than
the seen. The Unknown Deity, shrouded in im-
mensity from the reach of human thought, was
the first link of the chain of spiritual existences
which led through the Father and the Son,
and through beings further removed from per-
fection to Achamoth—a being imperfect enough
to give birth to this present imperfect material
universe. Such, in few words, was the poetic
and daring system of Valentinus, the most
Gnostic of the Gnostics.

Yet Gnosticism had its work. When the
fever of its excesses was past, it left the Church
more spiritual than it found it. The Christian
philosophers of Alexandria, Clement and Origen,
succeeded the Gnostic teachers, and taught the
Church to look for the deeper meaning of the
Bible, and in that deeper apprehension of it to
take a wider view of the world, its meaning,
and its destiny. This mention of Gnosticism is
necessary, for Gnosticism is a witness to the
Four Gospels, as we shall see when we come to
the testimony of Irenæus of Lyons.

D

MONTANISM.

Besides Gnosticism, I must mention one other great tendency, sectarian rather than heretical, which arose in the second century. To the free missionary activity of the apostles' days succeeded the more mechanical consolidating action of the sub-apostolic period. The Church found herself governed by aged men whose chief qualification was that they were old enough to have had intercourse in younger days with apostles. There was a great danger that Christian life would become stereotyped and that Christianity itself would become a past glory rather than a present power.

Then Montanus arose in Phrygia, a province of Asia Minor. Like the so-called " Quakers" of later times, he called attention to the almost forgotten truth that Christ had sent the Spirit at Pentecost to abide with the Church for ever. Christians were living in the times of the "Comforter" (Paraclete), and His voice was still to be heard through His prophets and prophetesses.

Montanus claimed for himself and for his followers, including two women, the gift of prophecy; the Church of Asia Minor cried blasphemy, and cast them out. Yet the prophesyings continued, and some were reduced to writing, and read for edification at the Montanist meetings. What, then, it will be asked, was the attitude of this sect towards the books of the New Testament?

Montanists and Catholics, so our evidence shows, were practically at one with regard to the Four Gospels. It may be said, in the first place, that the Montanist doctrine of the Comforter is either derived from S. John's Gospel, or else is an independent testimony to the teaching of the Gospel. It must certainly not be thought that the Gospel may, on the contrary, have proceeded from the Montanists, for there is equally early, or rather, perhaps, earlier evidence that it was used by the Gnostics, whose tendency was a wholly different one from that of the Montanists. A work proceeding from one of these bodies could hardly have been accepted by the other. Spiritualizers, like the Gnostics who explained away the resurrection of the body, had too little in common with men like the Montanists, who earnestly expected Christ's reign of a thousand years with His saints on earth; Gnostic and Montanist could receive in common only that which was earlier than both Gnosticism and Montanism.

The agreement between Catholics and Montanists as to the Gospels is emphasized by the evidence to be derived from Tertullian, the earliest and perhaps the only Montanist writer whose works are preserved. Writing about 210 A.D., he not only mentions that our Four Gospels were received by all the great Churches of the Christian World, but also specially occupies himself to show—and, indeed, he does show—that our Gospel of S. Luke is earlier than the recension of it adopted by Marcion the Gnostic (circ. 140 A.D.).

It has been said by some that the idea of a Canon—*i.e.* of a fixed collection of sacred writings definitely including certain books and definitely excluding all others—arose in the Church from conscious opposition to the Montanists, and that the limits of the Canon were fixed with an eye to exclude the writings of the Montanist prophets. Be this as it may be, one great fact remains unshaken; Catholic and Montanist were agreed that our Four Gospels, and none other than these, were to be received as authoritative and apostolic.

CHAPTER II.

Antioch (Theophilus)—Alexandria (Clement)—Lyons
(Irenæus).

WE now come to the question, what was the
history of the Four Gospels during the second
century? Can we show that they were known,
used, referred to as authorities in the second
century as they undoubtedly were in the third?

It will give point to these inquiries if we give
at once the substance of some other inquiries
which led to a very different result from the one
we hope to reach. We refer to a book called
"Supernatural Religion"; not because of any
knowledge we possess that the author, in spite
of evidence recently discovered, would still stand
by all that he wrote in 1879, but because he has
stated his view in vigorous English which is

remembered and repeated long after it has been once read.

His conclusions with regard to the Gospels may be thus summed up—

(*a*) No trace of our Gospels of S. Matthew, S. Mark, and S. John between 30 and 180 A.D.

(*b*) The Gospel of S. Luke allowed to have existed before 140 A.D., but not as a work of any authority.

(*c*) The Gospel according to the Hebrews and other lost Gospels asserted to have been the Gospels used between 95 and 170 A.D.

We have two great questions to ask with regard to these conclusions—

1. Are they true?

2. If they are true, how far are they important?

We must begin our inquiry at the earliest period at which it is generally agreed that our Gospels existed and were of authority in the Church. This period consists of the twenty or thirty years following 180 A.D., the date up to which the author of "Supernatural Religion" concludes that there is no trace of the Gospels of S. Matthew, S. Mark, and S. John.

If the conclusion be true, we have a remarkable

transformation scene as soon as we pass the year 180 A.D. At all the great centres of Christianity existing in the second century, we find, after the year 180 A.D., overwhelming evidence, not only of the existence of all four of our Gospels, but also of the reverence in which they were held, and of the authority attributed to them.

Let *Antioch* be mentioned first, because no other city is more closely connected with the earliest history of Christianity. About the year 180 A.D. Theophilus, the bishop there, wrote an "Apology for Christianity" to convince a heathen friend. In such a work many appeals to the Christian Scriptures are not to be expected, especially as the work is not a long one, but in it are quoted, besides some passages from S. Matthew, two verses of the first chapter of S. John, with the information added for the sake of his friend, that they were written by an inspired man named John.

So we have in the oldest Christian city (save Jerusalem) the Gospel of S. John, by all allowed to be the latest written of the Four Gospels, quoted as an inspired authority about the year 180 A.D. But books do not step into a

position of authority all at once, and in the light
of this fact (and of some others to be produced
later on), I venture to think that if no trace can
be found of the existence of S. John's Gospel
before 180 A.D. the circumstance is purely
accidental.

Let us pass southward next to Egypt. During
the period we are discussing, and both before
and after it, Alexandria was one of the five or
six great centres of Christianity. It is a good
place to go to for information. It is near Palestine, the scene of the events narrated in the
Gospels. It was celebrated for its learned men,
Christian as well as heathen. The man we shall
question here is the great writer Clement, at
this time head of the Catechetical School, *i.e.*
of the Christian Institute at which educated
heathen inquirers were received and furnished
with information regarding Christianity.

Clement was a really learned man. He could
quote Homer and the Tragedians, and had
Mythology at his fingers' ends. He could
understand and appreciate Greek philosophy.
Indeed, he declares that God gave the Greeks
philosophy as He gave the Jews the Law, to be
a schoolmaster to bring them to Christ. He

knew many Christian writings which are lost to us, and at times refers to them.

But his attitude towards the Four Gospels is unmistakable, as the following table shows. (Let us take fifty consecutive pages from a work addressed to *Christians*, for we do not find, and do not expect to find the same unrestrained readiness to quote Christian Scriptures in a work addressed to heathens).

Quotations in Clement of Alexandria (fifty consecutive pages of "Pædagogus," T. and T. Clark's Translation.)

From Old Testament	...	...	62
„ Gospels	...	...	...	52
„ Epistles	...	...	...	31
„ Classics	...	...	...	3

Thus it is seen that Clement quotes from one or other of the Four Gospels on every page on an average, besides frequently quoting the Old Testament and the Epistles.

If, however, something besides statistics is desired, take his witness in his own words. After giving a saying of our Lord not found in the Canonical Gospels, he adds, " We have not the saying in the Four Gospels which have been handed down to us, but in that according to the

E

Egyptians." Who does not feel, in reading this sentence, that Clement is warning his readers that he gives them a saying on an authority less generally accepted than that of the Canonical Gospels?

Clement died about 220 A.D., so this sentence was probably written before that year. Is it conceivable that by going back about thirty or forty years further we reach a time at which there is actually no trace of the existence of three out of four of the Gospels which Clement describes as "handed down to us" (*i.e.* to Christians at large)? If it be so, surely the absence of traces must be accidental. Moreover, such strong testimony at so early a date makes us feel that a careful search is likely to be rewarded by the discovery of still earlier traces which have been overlooked. It is becoming difficult to believe that there are none.

But we will have one more witness to the state of things existing *after* the magic year 180, before we go back to an earlier time. Irenæus, Bishop of Lyons in 180 A.D., is too important a witness to pass by. In spiritual descent, he was of the third generation only from the Lord Himself. Christ taught S. John, S. John taught

Polycarp of Smyrna, and Polycarp of Smyrna taught Irenæus of Lyons.

"I can describe," writes Irenæus,[1] "the very place in which the blessed Polycarp used to sit . . . and how he would describe his intercourse with John and with the rest who had seen the Lord. . . . And whatsoever things he had heard from them about the Lord, and about His miracles, and about His teaching, Polycarp would relate altogether in accordance with the Scriptures."

Here we plainly have a man who is in the full stream of the earliest Christian tradition. Further, he is independent of the last two witnesses; for he drew his Christianity, not from Antioch or Alexandria, but from Western Asia Minor, where S. Paul had laboured and S. John had died. The evidence of such a man as to the use of the Gospels in the Church, and the authority attributed to them, is plainly worth having. Let us have it. In fifty consecutive pages of his works [2] there are seventy quotations from our Gospels, many of them from S. John, together with a great number of quotations from the Old Testament and from the Epistles. Thus

[1] "Ad Florinum," Lightfoot, p. 95.   [2] Bk. iv., init.

there can be no possible doubt what books
Irenæus means when he says *Gospels*. Nor is
it doubtful how much authority he attributes
to them. He writes[1]:—

"So firm is the ground upon which these
Gospels rest that the very heretics themselves
bear witness to them, and starting from these
documents, each one of them endeavours to
establish his own peculiar doctrine. For the
Ebionites who use S. Matthew's Gospel only
are confuted out of this very same (of) making
false suppositions with regard to the Lord.
But Marcion, mutilating that according to Luke,
is proved to be a blasphemer of the only existing God from those passages which he still
retains. Those, again, who separate Jesus from
Christ, alleging that Christ remained impassible,
but that it was Jesus who suffered; preferring
the Gospel by Mark, if they read it with a
love of truth may have their errors rectified.
Those, moreover, who follow Valentinus (the
Gnostic), making copious use of that according
to John, to illustrate their conjunctions, shall
be proved to be totally in error by means of
this very Gospel."

[1] "Hær.," III., xi. 7. T. and T. Clark, p. 292.

Thus writes Irenæus about the year 190 A.D., and we can hardly exaggerate the importance of his testimony. He was no recluse, and though he lived in Gaul, we cannot call him a merely local witness. He kept up intercourse with Rome and the East till the end of the century. He showed on one great occasion his statesman-like care for the whole Church both in East and West. The dispute in the Christian Church with regard to the proper time at which Easter should be kept, had reached an acute stage. The Bishop of Rome made things still more unpleasant by excommunicating one side. A leading part in restoring peace fell to Irenæus.

Such is the man who bears witness that, about the year 190 A.D., and, no doubt, for some time before, our Four Gospels were so well established as to be acknowledged by Catholics and heretics as a common authority in controversy. What are we, then, to make of the statement that there is no trace of the very existence of three of them before 180 A.D. ? Surely these great authorities cannot have been made up in 180 A.D., and immediately accepted by all parties!

Let it then be placed on record that, at the earliest date after apostolic times, at which we have a Christian literature, wide in scope and large in bulk, and consisting chiefly of works addressed to Christians, we have overwhelming evidence that our Four Gospels were current from Antioch in the East, to Lyons in the West, and were looked upon as the great authoritative documents of the Christian Faith.

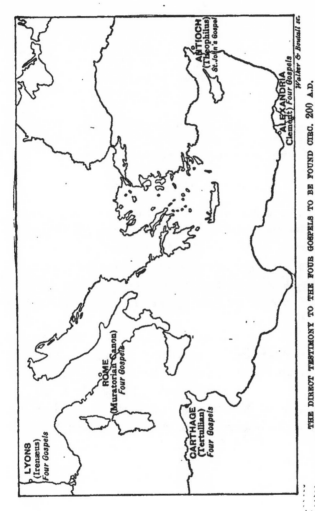

THE DIRECT TESTIMONY TO THE FOUR GOSPELS TO BE FOUND CIRC. 200 A.D.

Walker & Boutall sc.

LYONS
(Irenaeus)
Four Gospels

ROME
(Muratorian Canon)
Four Gospels

CARTHAGE
(Tertullian)
Four Gospels

ANTIOCH
(Theophilus)
St. John's Gospel

ALEXANDRIA
Clement) *Four Gospels*

NOTE I.—The "Muratorian Canon" is a list—perhaps the earliest list—of the Canonical Books of the New Testament.
NOTE II.—Spain, Britain, and Germany are not included, because so little is known of Christianity in those countries before 200 A.D.

CHAPTER III.

THE WITNESS OF TATIAN (160–180 A.D.).

Tatian's Life—His Apology—His "Diatessaron."

WE now leave the undisputed period (180–220 A.D.), and enter upon a time during which the author of "Supernatural Religion" tells us he found *no trace* of any of our Four Gospels except the third. In spite of his ill-success, we will venture on the same ground, in hope of finding what he missed.

The first witness to be examined is Tatian the Assyrian, the fellow-worker and disciple of Justin Martyr. The two facts, (1) that he was a fellow-worker with Justin, (2) that Irenæus [1] speaks of him in the past tense, go to show that he belonged to an earlier generation than Irenæus himself, but exact evidence of his date is wanting.

[1] "Hær.," I., 28.

Tatian was a rough mountaineer from beyond the Tigris, perhaps from the district in which the Archbishop of Canterbury's Mission to the Eastern Syrians (the so-called Nestorians) is now working. Like many others at that time, *i.e.* about 140 or 150, he came westward, ultimately to Rome, in search of truth. But the Greeks disgusted him by their pedantry, and, it must be confessed, by laughing at his failure to attain an Attic purity of accent; while the Romans sickened his healthy provincial soul by their exhibitions of gladiators. The sequel may be told in his own words:—

"As I was earnestly considering this, I came across certain barbarian writings, older in point of antiquity than the doctrines of the Greeks, and far too divine to be marked with their errors. What persuaded me in these books was the simplicity of the language . . . the noble explanation of creation, the predictions of the future, the excellence of the precepts, and the assertion of the government of all by one Being."

Tatian is a most important witness. He was generally reckoned, at least in his later career, as a heretic, so that his agreement with Catholic writers such as Irenæus on the subject of the

F

Gospels, if such agreement be found, must be reckoned as confirmation from an *independent*, if not from a *hostile* source.

Further, he spent many years at Rome, which was, in his time, already fast becoming the head-quarters of Christianity. At some time or other nearly all the great leaders of the Church, Ignatius, Polycarp, Irenæus, Marcion and other heretics, found their way to Rome. It was the place above all others where information about the faith and practice of Christians was to be obtained.

Tatian's evidence for the Gospels must be extracted from his two works, (1) "Oration to the Greeks," (2) "Diatessaron," or Harmony of Four Gospels.

The Oration is a short work, and is addressed to heathens; so that we must not expect to find the Christian Scriptures often quoted, or quoted at length. But we find two or three short sentences which, taken together, are very significant: cap. iv., "God is a Spirit;" cap. xiii., "The darkness doth not comprehend the light;" cap. xix., "All things were made by Him, and without Him was not anything made."

From these quotations, we may feel morally

certain that the writer had either seen S. John's Gospel, or, at least, heard it read; and we shall feel the more disposed to receive reasonable evidence that he used this Gospel among others in composing " The Diatessaron " (cf. J. M. Fuller, in Dict. Chr. Biog., *Tatian*).

" THE DIATESSARON."

We now come to " The Diatessaron." It is generally acknowledged that this work was written either in Syriac, Tatian's native language, or in Greek, the language in which he composed his Apology. Unfortunately no " Diatessaron " in Greek or Syriac is extant, and therefore we cannot at once say what Gospels were used.

But though it is impossible to say off-hand, it is not difficult to learn by inquiry. The first witness is *Eusebius*, the great Church historian, who wrote about the year 324 A.D., under the Emperor Constantine. He says rather contemptuously [1]—

" Tatian put together somehow a certain combination and collection of the Gospels and called

[1] " H. E.," iv. 29

it 'The Diatessaron.'[1] It is still current even
now in some quarters."

To estimate this statement at its true value,
we must remember that Eusebius was in many
ways the Bishop Lightfoot of the fourth century. His knowledge of early Christian literature was immense. He was no mean linguist,
for he knew Hebrew, Syriac, and Greek; and
if he stumbled in translating the knotty Latin
epigrams of Tertullian, he was not the last man
to do so. Further, he was a real critic. Nothing
makes him more angry than a foolish story
found in any of his authorities. He can tell
the difference between a fact and an inference
from a fact in the writers he uses, and in some
notable instances he draws his own inferences,
differing from those writers.

Again, he is fair, though he sometimes gets
impatient. His style is mainly straightforward,
though a little difficult; and if he becomes
turgid when he describes the sufferings of the
martyrs, Christians living in the comfortable
nineteenth century may forgive overstrained
eloquence in a man who went to prison for
Christ.

---

[1] *i.e.* "The Book of the Four."

Eusebius's testimony in the present case is precise ; it amounts to this—

Tatian composed his work from our Gospels, and called it "The Book of the Four," because all four of our evangelists were used.

But it has been suggested, from the carelessness with which Eusebius mentions "The Diatessaron," that he had never seen it, and so might be utterly mistaken about it. We cannot prove that the historian had seen it; but the title is a striking one, and unlikely to be a mistake. We will call the next witness.

Theodoret, a great Biblical commentator and a scholar as great as Eusebius, was bishop in Syria about the year 430 A.D., and was a neighbour, if not a fellow-countryman, of Tatian. His testimony is as follows [1]—

"Tatian also composed the Gospel called ' The Diatessaron,' removing the genealogies and all the other passages which show that Christ was born of David according to the flesh. This was used, not only by the members of his party, but even by those who followed the apostolic doctrine, as they did not perceive the evil design of the composition, but used the book in their simplicity for its conciseness."

[1] "Hær. Fab.," i. 20.

He then goes on to say that he found two hundred such books in use, and that he removed them from the churches, and substituted for them the Four Gospels.

From this testimony, it is clear (1) that Theodoret had seen Tatian's work; (2) that it was called still in his day "Diatessaron," the fourfold work; (3) that he quarrelled with it, because in it our Gospels were abbreviated in the interest of heresy, as he supposed.

So Eusebius is confirmed by a writer who was well qualified by his learning and place of residence to state the truth on the matter. But we will call the next witness.

Dionysius bar Salibi, a Syriac writer of the twelfth century, says that Tatian's work commenced with the opening words of S. John's Gospel. If the latest of the Gospels was used, surely the synoptics were not left out.

So the case stood when the author of "Supernatural Religion" issued his complete edition in 1879. But since then the libraries have been giving up their dead. The case now stands thus:

(i.) We have, in an Armenian version, a commentary (attributed to S. Ephraem) on a Gospel harmony. It is natural to believe that this is the commentary of S. Ephraem on Tatian's "Diatessaron," mentioned by Bar Salibi. The impression is confirmed by the fact that we discover from the commentary that the harmony began, as Bar Salibi says Tatian's "Diatessaron" began, with the opening words of S. John's Gospel. Moreover, on what harmony should Ephraem the Syrian comment, but on the harmony so widely used in the Syrian Church? We conclude, then, that we possess a commentary on "The Diatessaron" of Tatian, written only about two hundred years after "The Diatessaron" itself.

From the commentary, we can gain a good deal of knowledge about the text commented on. We cannot reconstruct the "Diatessaron," for the commentary is too unequal, sometimes running into little essays, sometimes barely referring to whole paragraphs, or skipping them altogether. But one thing is clear; the matter commented on is drawn from our Gospels, including that according to S. John. Additions from other sources are trifling.

An example will show the justice of these two statements. The commentary is divided into twenty-two chapters, in each of which the matter commented on agrees with the substance of our Gospels, and the wording (when given) is, with slight exceptions, the wording of our Gospels. Since, however, some selection must be made, we choose that part of the commentary which refers to the crucifixion as our example.

Separating, then, from the body of the commentary the Gospel quotations upon which Ephraem comments, we get the following passages. We leave it to the reader to decide whether they are drawn from our Gospels or not. For purposes of comparison, we add references to our Gospels, at the same time underlining any variation. Some allowance must of course be made for the usual inaccuracy in form of all ancient quotations.

1. "And when He had taken up His cross and gone forth, they found and laid hold of a certain man of Cyrene, and they laid upon him the cross" (John xix. 17, and Luke xxiii. 26).

2. "If they do this in a green tree" (Luke xxiii. 31).

3. "That the saying might be accomplished, He was reckoned with the unjust" (Mark xv. 28, a verse relegated to the margin of the Revised Version).

4. "This is *Christ* the King of the Jews" (Matt. xxvii. 37).

5. "*If* Thou art the Christ, save Thyself and us *with Thee*" (Luke xxiii. 39).

6. "Remember me, Lord, in Thy kingdom" (Luke xxiii. 42).

7. "To-day thou shalt be with Me in the *garden of Pleasure*"[1] (Luke xxiii. 43).

8. "And they gave Him to drink vinegar *and gall*" (Matt. xxvii. 48).

9. "Woe, woe to us, this was the Son of God; the judgment of the destruction of Jerusalem is come" (cf. Luke xxiii. 48, and especially the new fragment of the "Gospel of Peter," which reads, "Then the Jews and the elders and the priests began to lament and to say, Woe to our sins; the judgment draweth near and the end of Jerusalem").

10. "My God, my God, why hast Thou forsaken me" (Matt. xxvii. 46).

11. "Let us see whether Elias cometh to take Him down" (Mark xv. 36).

12. "He saved others; Himself He cannot save" (Matt. xxvii. 42).

[1] This may be simply the equivalent in Armenian for "Paradise."

13. "Into Thy hands I commend My spirit"
(Luke xxiii. 46).

14. "One of the soldiers smote Him with a
spear (*lanceâ*") (John xix. 34).

(ii.) We have in the next place a newly discovered Arabic work professing to be a translation of Tatian's "Diatessaron." This claim is
strengthened by the fact that the arrangement
of at least the opening chapters agrees with
the arrangement witnessed to by Ephraem's
commentary.

(iii.) We have an anonymous harmony edited
in the sixth century by Victor of Capua, who
believed it to be "The Diatessaron" of Tatian.
This, if Tatian's, has certainly been added to
and altered, for it contains the genealogies, and
begins with the opening words of S. Luke's
Gospel. On the other hand, it follows Tatian's
plan of weaving the Gospels into a connected
story. On the whole, it is safest to assume that
it is based on Tatian.

There is, however, an objection which forbids
us to identify even the Arabic harmony in its
present state with the original "Diatessaron."
Tatian's work was short as compared with the
Four Gospels, for Theodoret says that it was

used on account of its *conciseness.* On the
other hand, this. Arabic harmony is not considerably shorter than the text of the Four
Gospels. To reconstruct Tatian from the Latin
and Arabic would be a hopeless task.

But fortunately our task is not reconstruction,
but simply to inquire from what source Tatian
drew his materials. If we begin our inquiries
with the two harmonies at present extant,
which are ascribed to Tatian, we find that each
contains the bulk of the text of the Four
Gospels, and very little indeed besides.

What then is the safest conclusion to draw
with regard to the original work on which these
two harmonies were based ? Surely that a book
which tempted copyists to insert so much material from our Gospels was originally a brief
compilation from our Gospels. Transcribers
missed the context of Tatian's extracts, and
supplied it freely from the original work, *i.e.*
that of the four evangelists.

The foregoing conclusion becomes inevitable
when the rest of the evidence is taken into
consideration. An examination of the extant
harmonies, a study of Ephraem's commentary,
and the testimony of Eusebius, Theodoret, and

Bar Salibi,—these three independent lines of evidence lead alike to the conclusion that Tatian used our Four Gospels in compiling "The Diatessaron." Evidence of his use of a fifth Gospel is too slight to be worthy of consideration.

CHAPTER IV.

THE WITNESS OF JUSTIN MARTYR (150 A.D.).

A sketch of Justin Martyr's life and qualifications as a witness—His evidence with regard to S. Matthew and S. Luke.

OUR next witness carries us some fifteen or twenty years further back, *i.e.* to circ. 150 A.D. At Rome, about that time, we find the most interesting man of his age, Justin Martyr the Philosopher, defending Christianity in an Apology addressed to the Emperor Antoninus Pius, and assailing the teaching of Marcion, the most Christian of the Gnostics. Justin was born in Palestine within a century, perhaps, of the birth of the Christ Himself.

He was a Greek by origin, and began his search for truth with the study of Greek philosophy. He found a Stoic teacher unsatisfying, and a Peripatetic too eager for fees. He next applied to a Pythagorean for teaching, but the Pythagorean excluded him by a sort of entrance examination in music, astronomy, and geometry. At last, in Platonism, he thought to find what he sought, "a clear vision of God." But a rival stronger than Platonism finally won him. "I found Christianity," he writes, "the only philosophy that is sure, and suited to man's wants." Like his predecessor, S. Paul, he came to Rome as an ambassador for Christ, and, like S. Paul, he died there a martyr's death.

Justin was, as we have seen, Tatian's teacher, and Tatian, as we have seen, used our Four Gospels. Is there not, then, some presumption— of a low degree, perhaps—that Justin himself used them?

Justin appeals to writings which he calls, "Memoirs of the Apostles." He says they were called, "Gospels," and that they were written by apostles and those who followed them. Is not this the way in which we should describe *our* Four Gospels, two of them being ascribed to the apostles S. Matthew and S. John, and two of them to followers of the apostles, S. Mark and S. Luke? Does not our first presumption rise in the scale of probability?

But what was the substance of Justin's Gospel? What facts does he mention?

"He tells us that Christ was descended from Abraham through David; that the angel Gabriel was sent to foretell His birth to the Virgin Mary—that this was a fulfilment of the prophecy of Isaiah—that Joseph was forbidden in a vision to put away his *espoused* wife; that our Saviour's birth at Bethlehem had been foretold by Micah; that His parents went thither from Nazareth where they dwelt, in consequence of the enrolment (taxing) under Cyrenius; that as they could not find a lodging in the village, they lodged in a cave close by it, where Christ was born, and laid by Mary in a manger; that while there, wise men from Arabia, guided by a star, worshipped Him, and offered Him gold, and frankincense, and myrrh."

Shall we continue? or may we take it for granted that we *have* found a trace of two at least of our Gospels? though Justin not only wrote before the year 180 A.D., but, according to some authorities, may even have died before 150 A.D.

No, we must not take it for granted, for it is urged that it was not our Gospels which were used, but some other or others. Justin's quotations have been placed side by side with the corresponding passages from our Gospels, and we are assured that *our* Gospels cannot be the source of the quotations.

The case stands thus. We find in Justin a mass of Gospel sayings in which slight verbal variations from the text of our Gospels are very frequent; while, on the other hand, any difference in substance is hardly to be found. There is, however, nothing extraordinary in this verbal variation. Other Fathers, later than Justin, who, without doubt, used our Gospels, are inaccurate in their quotations. It is worth while, on this topic, to cite the words of a writer, not on the Canon, but on the "Textual Criticism of the New Testament."

"A physical cause," writes Dr. Warfield (p. 74), "lies at the bottom of much of the looseness of patristic quotation. There were no handy reference Bibles in those days, no concordances, no indices; and books were dear, and not at all times within reach. For brief quotations, memory was necessarily relied on; and thus the habit of depending on memory fixed itself. Even very long quotations can often be but little trusted in their details," etc.

But it is necessary to come to particulars. In chapters 15–17 of "Apology," I., we find a kind of abstract of our Lord's moral teaching presented, that the Emperor might see how pure a morality the Christians taught. It is a natural supposition that Justin would cast this abstract into a form of his own ; and, if so, we must not be surprised to find the order and wording a little different from the order and wording of our Gospels, even if he used our Gospels.

In "Apology," I., c. 15, we have the following, which is a fair specimen of Justin's quotations. (For convenience, it is divided into six sections).

(The Christ) said thus :—

1. " To every one that asketh give ye, and from him that desireth to borrow, turn not ye away " (Matt. v. 42).

2. " For if ye lend to those from whom ye hope to receive " (Luke vi. 34).

3. " What new thing do ye ? This even the publicans do " (Matt. v. 46 and 47).

4. " But ye, lay not up for yourselves treasures upon the earth, where moth and rust doth corrupt and robbers break through ; but lay up for yourselves treasures in the heavens,

H

where neither moth nor rust corrupteth " (Matt. vi. 19, 20).

5. " For what is a man profited, if he gain the whole world, but lose his soul? Or what shall he give in exchange for it ? " (Matt. xvi. 26).

6. "Therefore lay up treasures in the heavens, where neither moth nor rust doth corrupt" (Matt. vi. 19).

Now, comparing the parts of the above quotation with the passages from our Gospels to which references are given, we find: (1) no difference in sense, (2) no difference in wording beyond such variations as "new thing" (Justin), " extra thing" (S. Matt.); " robbers "(Justin), "thieves" (S. Matt.); "lose his soul" (Justin), " be mulcted of his soul" (S. Matt.).

It is difficult to believe on the ground of differences so slight that Justin used a Gospel different from any of ours; but if it was so, then Justin's Gospel must have been at least as much like our Synoptic Gospels as they are like one another, and our loss of a fifth Gospel is not a serious one.

But one argument remains to be dealt with. A glance at the references to chapter and verse appended to the different parts of the quotation makes it seem unlikely that a man *looking out his passages in a copy of our Gospels* would skip about so much.

But the question is, Is it likely that Justin would copy out his quotations straight from his authorities ? We have already seen, from Dr. Warfield's words, that it is unlikely that the Fathers generally would do such a thing. In Justin's case, there are two additional reasons why it is probable that he quoted merely from memory : (1) in the first place, he was writing for heathens for whom it was sufficient to give the general sense; (2) in the second place, his quotations from the Old Testament (and they are many) show a similar inaccuracy in wording.

A *defective memory* will explain all the variations of the passage chosen for consideration ("Apology," I., xv.). Now, Justin's memory can hardly have been good; he was a heathen till he was grown up, and so had not learned the Gospels with the retentive memory of childhood. Further, the passage is a representative one ; the difficulties it presents are not less than those to be found elsewhere ; the solution which satisfies them is satisfactory also in most other cases. Only here and there does another hypothesis seem more probable, viz. that Justin alters obscure expressions that the heathen may better understand them.

We conclude, that if human nature is human nature in all ages as well as in all climes, Justin Martyr used our Gospels, and would have been greatly astonished to be told he had not.

CHAPTER V.

THE WITNESS OF HERMAS (circ. 140–150 A.D.).

"The Shepherd "—Its symbolism a veiled witness to the Fourfold Gospel.

THERE is one curious piece of evidence in favour
of our Four Gospels which was recently brought
to light by Dr. Taylor,[1] Master of S. John's
College, Cambridge. Among the writings of the
Apostolic Fathers is generally reckoned a work
called "The Shepherd," written by one Hermas.
The author was formerly supposed to be the
Hermas to whom S. Paul sends greeting in the
Epistle to the Romans. It is perhaps owing to
this identification that "The Shepherd" was in-
cluded among the works of the Apostolic Fathers.
This identification is now generally given up in

[1] In the Cambridge *Journal of Philology* for January, 1890.
See also "The Witness of Hermas to the Four Gospels"
(1892), by the same author.

the face of the precise statement of a second-
century author who wrote at Rome; for the
author of the Muratorian Fragment declares that
Hermas wrote "The Shepherd" while "his brother
Pius" was Bishop of Rome. "The Shepherd,"
then, is a Roman document, dating circ. 140–
150 A.D., and could not have proceeded from a
contemporary of S. Paul. On the other hand,
it is at least as early as the "Apology" of Justin
Martyr, and possibly earlier.

Now, we found in Justin clear traces of the
use of our Gospels of S. Matthew and S. Luke,
or, at least, of Gospels closely resembling them
both in wording and contents. In Hermas we
meet with quite different phenomena; we have
apparent allusions to our Gospels, and many
phrases and statements which remind us of
them; but, on the other hand, we find hardly
anything which could be called a quotation from
either Canonical or Uncanonical Gospels.

As an example of an apparent allusion, we
notice that Hermas is shown in a vision a new
gate, "which was made new, that those who are
about to be saved might enter in thereby into
the kingdom of God" (Sim. ix. 12. 3). He is
told that the gate is the Son of God. It is not

unreasonable to find in these words a reference·
to S. John x. 9, " I am the *door ;* by Me if any
man enter in, he shall be saved." But we
acknowledge that this and other apparent references, when taken alone, would fall short of
proving that Hermas was acquainted with our
Gospels.

The really valuable evidence to be derived
from Hermas is of a different kind from that to
be derived from Justin, and forms a valuable
supplement to it. Hermas seems to say nothing
less than this, viz. that in his own time, *i.e.* as
early as 140–150 A.D., and perhaps still earlier,
there existed at Rome an authoritative collection of *Four* Gospels. If he really says this,
his evidence is of the highest value. These Four
Gospels must be *our* four, because there is no
trace in East or West of any other Gospels
which ever formed a collection of four.

But there must be a history behind the collection. People collect things which have already,
by lapse of time and by practical proof, gained a
certain value or authority. Coins are collected
only after they have become valuable or old.
Laws are collected into codes after they have
been tried and found useful. In like manner,

our Four Gospels must have individually. gained respect or authority before they were formed into a collection. If Dr. Taylor has rightly interpreted Hermas, he has proved that as early as 140–150 A.D., *each* of our Four Gospels had an honourable history behind it.

A little patience and care will be well bestowed in following Dr. Taylor's argument. Unless it be borne in mind that the ways of the second century are not the ways of the nineteenth, the interpretation of Hermas to be given may seem forced, or even impossible.

The most earnest of the early Christians, on their conversion, found their outer lives narrowed in proportion as their inner lives were enlarged. The amphitheatre and the circus, literature and art, appeared to such men as Athens had appeared to S. Paul, "wholly given to idolatry" (R.V., "full of idols"). They renounced them all. But Nature reasserted her sway; the rude beginnings of a new art and new literature manifested themselves in Christianity itself. Art showed itself in the symbolic figures scratched on the walls of the catacombs, literature in imaginative works like "The Shepherd" of Hermas.

"The Shepherd" was meant to be both religious and interesting. It has been compared
to Bunyan's "Pilgrim's Progress;" but there is
a strong contrast between the two works. The
"Pilgrim" is a story, the interest of which depends on the fortunes of its lifelike characters;
"The Shepherd" is an allegory, which keeps our
interest in proportion as the meaning is "half-
revealed and half-concealed." We must remember this fact in interpreting the language
of Hermas.

The book begins with a threefold vision of
very simple structure. In the first vision,
Hermas sees an aged woman sick unto death,
seated in a *chair*, the seat of teaching and
authority. She reads to him terrible words
out of a book, an allusion, possibly, to the Law
given on Sinai. This woman, we are told, represents the *Church*; may we conclude that she
represents the Jewish Church in possession of
the Law of Moses? At the end, she and her
chair are carried off to the East.

In the second vision, Hermas sees the same
woman, but she is partially restored. She walks,
reading a little book. Hermas mistakes her for
the Sibyl, a mystic, prophetic figure, in whose

I

name many predictions were current among the
early Christians, but he is told that she is the
Church. She is *more cheerful,* as one to whom
an inheritance has been left. She lends Hermas
the little book, but demands it back because the
revelation is not yet complete. May we not
take her as the figure of the Jewish Church in
possession of the promises of prophecy; not sitting teaching, but standing, because the Law is
destined to pass away, and the Gospel has not
yet come ?

In the third vision, Hermas sees again the
same woman, now young and fair, and "*joyous
as one to whom good tidings* have come." He
is told to mark that her position is firm because
she is sitting on a *bench* (*subsellium*); because
the bench has four feet, and stands firmly, *for
the world also is held together by the strength of
four elements.*

The woman tells six young men who are with
her to go and build; and presently Hermas sees
a great tower being built upon the waters. This
tower, she tells him, is herself—the Church—and
is built upon the waters, "because your life was
saved, and will be saved, by water" (probably
an allusion to baptism, for the same expression

is used in reference to baptism in 1 Pet. iii. 20, 21). At the end, she and the bench are carried off to the tower. Surely the application of the third vision is to the Church no longer Jewish, but Christian, because the Gospel has come. Thus we seem to have in these three visions—the Law, the Prophets, and the Gospel.

But we are in search of something more definite still, viz. the Four written Gospels. Is there any trace of these in the vision? Yes, in the figure of the bench with the four feet, answers Dr. Taylor. Let us, then, consider the language which Hermas uses with regard to the bench.

1. In the first place, the bench is something of great importance, belonging to the Church. It is the first thing which arrests the attention of Hermas during the third vision, and it is the last thing, the significance of which is explained to him by the Interpreter, who interprets all three visions at the close. When the woman is carried off to the tower which is building, the bench is carried after her, as though it denoted a permanent possession of the Church. Now, if it can be shown that the bench signifies the Four Gospels, it is clear how great was the

importance Hermas attributed to them. His
vision will then be proved to be a vision of the
Church and of the Gospels.

2. In the first vision, the chair (the word
used, S. Matt. xxiii. 2, "Moses' *seat*") appears
to represent the Mosaic Law. Nothing is said
in the interpretation with regard to the chair
except that it is suitable for one who is weak
through age. The relation of the Law to the
Jewish Church might well be so expressed by
a Christian writer of the second century. But
no attention is called to the number of feet, or
other parts, of the chair, probably because the
books in which the Law is contained, being five
in number, do not lend themselves to a numerical
analogy which would suit a chair. Nor is the
chair particularly interesting to the writer.

In the third vision, the bench takes the place
of the chair. The same figure could not be
used of two things between which so strong an
antithesis exists as between the Law and the
Gospel. In the case of the bench, attention is
called in the interpretation to the fact that it
has four feet. Why so in the case of the *bench*,
but not in the case of the *chair*? Surely it is
not unreasonable to conclude that the antitype

of the bench was in some sense fourfold, while
the antitype of the chair was not so. The one
bench may be regarded as representing the collection of the Four Gospels, just as the one chair
may represent the five books of Moses gathered
into one Torah.

3. The bench is that on which the Church
sits, the authority on which it rests. Why
should this authority be represented with
emphasis as fourfold ? It cannot be a reference
to the Saviour Himself, nor to His twofold
nature, nor to the Trinity, nor to the Twelve
Apostles, nor to the Orders of the Ministry.
There is nothing on which the Church has ever
rested, or seemed to rest, which could be
represented as a fourfold authority, except the
Canonical Gospels.

4. Lastly—and this is a most important point
—the Interpreter of the Vision finds it necessary to *apologize* for the fact that the authority
on which the Church depends is fourfold.

He tells Hermas to mark that the position
of the Church is "firm, because she is sitting
on a bench; because the bench has four feet,
and stands firmly." So far all is simple, and
the four feet might be merely a figure signi-

fying that the Church was firmly based, on what foundation it matters not. But the Interpreter does not stop here, but goes on to justify the number *four*. "The bench has four feet, and stands firmly, for the world also is held together by the strength of four elements." We must conclude, therefore, that some antitype of fourfold nature stands behind that "four." The four elements have to do, not with the bench, but with the antitype of the bench. The bench is firm, for the sufficient reason that it has four feet; but the thing signified by the bench is firm because it answers to the Constitution (as then understood) of Nature. Plainly, the antitype is something the fourfoldness of which needs justifying, and can only be justified by a far-fetched analogy with the four "elements"—fire, water, earth, and air.

Is not the Fourfold Gospel such an antitype? To answer this question, it must first be remarked that the fact of the existence of four Gospels proves from time to time a stumbling-block, especially to the unthinking. It would be simpler, they say, to have one Gospel. Certainly we should, in that case, be saved from some difficulties and discrepancies. On the other hand, we have, as it is, a great advantage; the Fourfold Gospel is fourfold testimony. But when once we try to prove that there is some special fitness in the number (four Gospels, rather than three or five), we are driven back on far-fetched analogies similar to the one which, as Dr. Taylor believes, meets us here. We conclude that the Fourfold Gospel may be reasonably identified with the antitype of the bench, the four feet of which are compared to the four "elements."

This conclusion would be greatly strengthened if it could be shown that such far-fetched analogies were used in reference to the Four Gospels at a time not far from the date of the composition of "The Shepherd." Now this is just what we can show. Irenæus of Lyons, writing about a generation and a half later than Hermas, in a well-known passage ("Hær.," III., 11. 11), says that there could be neither more nor fewer than four Gospels. For since there are four regions of the world and four winds, it was natural that the Church should have four pillars. The Word of God sits on the four-faced cherubim; the Son of God sits on the Four Gospels.

In this passage of Irenæus we get the far-fetched analogies between the Gospels and natural things; and we also find the Gospels represented as *supports*, as pillars on which the Church rests, as a *seat* on which Christ *sits*. If in the language of Irenæus, writing circ. 190 A.D., the Gospels are a *seat*, may not Hermas, writing circ. 140–150 A.D., mean the Gospels by his symbolic bench?

But there is probably a closer relationship between the two writers than the relationship of nearness in time. Irenæus, in one place, quotes a sentence found in "The Shepherd," with the introductory formula, "Well therefore said the Scripture which saith," etc. If we may draw the fullest inference from this, Irenæus knew the work of Hermas, and treated it as Scripture; and we may then further conclude that his analogies were suggested by "The Shepherd."

In conclusion, one objection may be mentioned; why did not Hermas himself explain the meaning of the bench, if it be significant? We answer, in the first place, that it is of the nature of his book to "half conceal and half reveal," and, in the second place, that the Four

Gospels were *so well* established in Hermas' time that any symbolism which included the number "four" must needs suggest them. It may be said that this is only an hypothesis, but it is an hypothesis which is rendered probable by the language of Irenæus regarding the Gospels.

From the whole of the foregoing evidence derived from "The Shepherd," the general conclusion to be drawn seems to us to be this: that in the time of Hermas at Rome, then (140–150 A.D.) fast becoming the head-quarters of Christianity, there were for Christians two, and only two, great facts, and that one of these was the Church, and the other our Four Gospels.

K

CHAPTER VI.

THE WITNESS OF PAPIAS (140–150 A.D.).

The witness of " The Elder " (circ. 100 A.D.), quoted by Papias, to S. Mark—The witness of Papias himself to S. Matthew.

WE next pass to a contemporary of Justin, Papias of Hierapolis, one of the cities of Western Asia Minor. Papias is important, not for himself, but because he collected the traditions of the earlier generations. Here is a testimony to S. Mark (a Gospel hitherto little noticed in these pages) given on the authority of " The Elder," *i.e.* probably *John* the Elder, a personal disciple of the Lord, and therefore hardly to be dated later than the year 100 A.D.

" Mark having become the interpreter of S. Peter, wrote down accurately all his (*i.e.* probably *Peter's*) reminiscences, without however recording in order what was either said or done by Christ. For neither did he hear the Lord, nor did he follow Him; but afterwards, as I said, attended Peter, who adapted his instructions to the needs of his hearers, but had no design of giving a connected account of the Lord's oracles (or discourses)."

Regarding the date of this testimony, there is no dispute, but many critics deny that it refers to our present Gospel of S. Mark. Our present Gospel, they say, is the most orderly of the three Synoptics, whereas the Gospel referred to by the Elder is described as not recording in order either the words or deeds of Christ.

There is a double answer to this argument of the critics: in the first place, the difficulty they point to is smaller than appears; in the second place, their solution raises a greater difficulty than it solves. The difficulty of identifying our S. Mark with the Elder's S. Mark is simply this: that the critics *consider* our Mark as orderly in its arrangement, while the Elder *considered* his S. Mark as not "recording in order." There is a difference of *opinion*, and therefore the critics conclude there is a difference of subject. As though a Christian of the first century and a critic of the nineteenth could not disagree on a matter of taste !

But was there no circumstance to predispose the Elder to find want of arrangement in S. Mark's Gospel? The Elder tells how it was composed from the sermons of S. Peter which did not form an orderly account of our Lord's life and teaching, though, without doubt, they embraced the most important features of the same. The Elder, under such circumstances, would not expect a strictly orderly arrangement of the matter.

Are there phenomena in our present S. Mark to justify this expectation? Certainly there are. S. Mark does not begin at the beginning with any account of the infancy of our Lord, nor does he give such data for chronology in the course of his Gospel as S. Luke gives in ch. iii., or as S. John gives by mentioning different Jewish feasts in connection with the events of the Ministry.

Further, the hypothesis of a lost S. Mark raises the difficulty, How came one Gospel to be lost and another to be substituted for it? It must have been lost either *before Papias* wrote, *or* between the date of Papias' work and the date of Irenæus (190 A.D.).

Was it lost before Papias wrote (140–150

A.D.)? The fragment of Papias quoted by
Eusebius, which is all we have, says nothing
about such a loss. Eusebius, who had the
whole work of Papias, says nothing. Irenæus,
who quotes from Papias, also says nothing.
Evidence is wanting for such a loss in Papias'
time.

But it is still more difficult to believe that
it disappeared after Papias wrote, and before
Irenæus composed his great work against all
heresies. In the first place, Irenæus, far from
telling us of any such disappearance of the
genuine work of S. Mark, reckons our S. Mark
among the Four Gospels, the authority of which,
he tells us, was so firmly established in the
Church that Catholic and heretic alike appealed
to them.

But a Gospel accepted by Papias could not be
superseded by a different one during the lifetime of Irenæus without Irenæus's knowledge.
Irenæus came from the same district as Papias
(Western Asia Minor); he was a disciple of
Papias' friend Polycarp, he had Papias' work
before him, he was in communication to the end
of his life with Western Asia Minor. How could
he help hearing of the substitution during his

own lifetime of another Gospel for the one known to Papias?

We conclude, then, that the testimony quoted by Papias from the Elder refers to our S. Mark. The importance of this testimony is very great, for it carries us back to a date not later than circ. 100 A.D., *i.e.* within forty years of the traditional date of the composition of the Gospel.

But Papias mentions by name not only a Gospel attributed to S. Mark, but also one attributed to S. Matthew. And here let us remark how fragmentary is the evidence for the use of the Gospels in the early Church. It reads like a few disjointed parts of a lost whole. The Gospels, with two exceptions, are not mentioned *by name* before circ. 190 A.D., the date at which Irenæus wrote. But these two exceptions are significant; the first bridges the way to the second, and the second carries us into the first century. About 140–150 A.D. (to take the latest reasonable date), Papias mentions a work (no doubt a Gospel) by S. Matthew; and about 90–100 A.D. (to take again the latest reasonable date), Papias' authority, John the Elder, tells how S. Mark wrote down S. Peter's reminiscences.

But let no one assume that the evidence always was and always will be as fragmentary as it is at present. The bulk of the literature of the second century is lost, and with it, one must believe, much that would have served as evidence—and may in the future serve as evidence—with regard to the authorship of the Gospels and their use in the early Church. Why, when so much was lost, should we suppose that every allusion of evidential value to our Gospels would have been preserved? Take the case of Eusebius, to whom far more than to any other writer we are indebted for the preservation of fragments of lost literature, and you will find that his quotations relate to matters of every kind, and by no means to the Gospels chiefly. Those which refer to the Gospels seem to have been preserved rather because they contained some interesting story than because they could be used as evidence on the subject which we are considering. Eusebius would see no reason for preserving fragments to prove that which for him and his contemporaries needed no proof, viz. the authority of the Four Gospels. With a mass of literature now lost to us before him, Eusebius wrote of our Canonical Gospels that first among the acknowledged books of the New Testament must be reckoned " The Holy Quaternion (fourfold work) of the Gospel" ("Eccl. Hist.," Bk. iii. c. 25).

To return now to Papias and his evidence with regard to S. Matthew. Eusebius ("Eccl. Hist.," Bk. iii. c. 39), after giving Papias' account of S. Mark, quoted from the same authority the following statement with regard to S. Matthew :—

" Matthew therefore wrote the sayings (*logia*) in Hebrew, and each one interpreted them as he was able."

We must notice in the first place that, as the word " therefore " shows, we have here a fragment torn from its context. We cannot tell what that context was, and hence we do not know whether the sayings referred to are the sayings of the Lord Himself, or whether they are the sayings current among Christians which recorded the words and works of the Lord. A collection of such sayings, "an oral gospel," must have existed before gospels were written, and it is conceivable at least that even an apostle may have drawn upon these materials in describing scenes at which he was not present,

or in refreshing his memory of things which he
had seen and heard.

The usual interpretation, however, given to
logia (sayings) is that of "sayings of the
Lord;" and from Papias' statement thus interpreted two important conclusions have been
drawn. It has been said, in the first place, that
Papias' S. Matthew consisted only of discourses
of our Lord, and so could not be the Hebrew
original of our Greek S. Matthew; and in the
second place, that Papias, writing as late as circ.
140–150 A.D., knew of no authoritative translation
of the Hebrew original written by S. Matthew.

But we must beware of drawing large conclusions from our tiny fragment. All that we can
do is to take its statements as they stand, and
inquire whether, as far as they go, they suit the
case of our present S. Matthew? Can we say
of the author of the Canonical Gospel, "Matthew
wrote the sayings [of the Lord] in Hebrew"?

That our S. Matthew was originally written
in Hebrew is asserted by Irenæus (190 A.D.) and
Origen (186–253 A.D.). Again, that our S.
Matthew wrote *the sayings* of the Lord is self-
evident. His Gospel is fuller of *logia* than that
of either of the two remaining synoptics.

S. Matthew is almost always summary
except when he is giving the sayings of the
Lord. After the first four chapters which contain only the sayings at the Baptism and
Temptation, we find three chapters wholly occupied with one great discourse, the Sermon on
the Mount. The eighth chapter contains several
miracles, but striking sayings occur in connection with three of them. The ninth chapter,
if full of incident, is also full of gracious sayings.
The four following chapters (x.–xiii.) contain
hardly anything besides charges to the Twelve,
parables, warnings addressed to the Pharisees,
and teaching of all kinds. The fourteenth is
a chapter of incidents; but half the fifteenth, and
the whole of the sixteenth, is given up to short
discourses. The short seventeenth chapter gives
the account of the Transfiguration, the healing
of the demoniac boy, and the payment of the
half-shekel; but these incidents lead up to
weighty sayings, viz. to a prophecy of the
Passion, to a eulogy on faith, and to an implicit
claim to Divine sonship. The three chapters
following (xviii.–xx.) contain chiefly answers to
hard questions. Chapter xxi. begins with the
triumphal entry into Jerusalem, but the remain-

ing three-fourths of the chapter are taken up
with parables and answers to questions. The
next four chapters (xxii.–xxv.) are occupied
with answers, denunciations of the Pharisees,
prophecies of the Advent, and parables. Chapter
xxvi. (the account of the Lord's Supper and the
Betrayal) is full of brief, significant sayings.
Chapter xxvii. (the trial before Pilate, and the
Crucifixion) is the only chapter in which perhaps
there are fewer sayings than one might expect,
e.g. only one of the last words is given. Finally,
the Gospel closes with the Lord's eternal message
to the Church—

" All authority is given Me in heaven and
upon earth. Go ye therefore, and make disciples
of all the nations. . . . Behold, I am with you
always."

Thus sixteen out of twenty-eight chapters
of our Greek Gospel of S. Matthew are given up
to sayings of our Lord, and in four others the
sayings are treated as of equal importance to
the incidents with which they are connected.
May we not, therefore, say of our S. Matthew
that "he wrote the sayings of the Lord " ?

That which Papias says, therefore, of the
Hebrew S. Matthew is true also of our Greek

Gospel; and the time at which the translation was made seems to me to be a question of minor importance. Still, it is just worth while remarking that Papias does *not* deny the existence of a generally accepted Greek translation in his own day. He says (using the past tense), "Each man translated them (*i.e.* the Lord's sayings as written down by S. Matthew) as he was able." If there were no Greek S. Matthew at the time at which Papias wrote, is it not evident that he would have said, "Each man translates them (*present tense*) as he is able" (*present tense again*)?

CHAPTER VII.

THE GOSPEL STORY.

The Apostolic Fathers (Clement of Rome, Ignatius of Antioch, Polycarp of Smyrna, Barnabas)—The four great Epistles of S. Paul.

By " Apostolic Fathers " I mean those Fathers who stood nearest in time to the apostles. The term is sometimes used vaguely, so it is well to say at once that in this book the title is restricted to the four writers, Clement of Rome (fl. circ. 96), Ignatius of Antioch (circ. 116), Polycarp of Smyrna (wrote circ. 116), and Barnabas (a different person from S. Paul's companion), who probably wrote before 120 A.D.

The probably genuine works of these writers to which only we appeal, are, one epistle of Clement to the Corinthians, seven epistles of Ignatius, one epistle of Polycarp, and one of Barnabas. The bulk of all taken together is very small; in Greek, they fill less than a hundred pages of ordinary size.

Speaking generally, the works of the Apostolic Fathers present the same phenomena as those of Justin as regards evangelic quotations, but the quotations are not so numerous. A characteristic example is the following. Polycarp (c. ii.) writes—

"Remembering that which the Lord said in His teaching: (*a*) 'Judge not, that ye be not judged;' (*b*) '(Forgive, and it shall be forgiven you;' (*c*) 'Be ye merciful, that ye may obtain mercy;' (*d*) 'With what measure ye mete, it shall be measured to you (again).' "

The words not in brackets are found in S. Matt. vii. 1, 2. Clauses (*b*) (*c*) seem to be modelled on (*a*); they are not to be found in either S. Matt. or S. Luke, but in their sense they may be compared with S. Luke vi. 37, 38 ("Release, and ye shall be released; give, and it shall be given unto you "). Clement of Rome (c. xiii.) writes—

"Remembering the words of the Lord Jesus which He spake in His teaching as to gentleness and longsuffering; for thus He said."

The quotation which follows contains in a slightly altered form the words given by Polycarp,

intermixed with three similar clauses in a form
differing both from Polycarp and the Gospels
(" As ye do, so shall it be done to you "). These
extra clauses contain no new thought.

The conclusions to be drawn from a consideration of these quotations are somewhat as
follows :—

1. Both quotations are a legitimate extension
and paraphrase for a preacher's purpose of two
clauses found in S. Matthew's Gospel (marked
(*a*) (*d*) in the quotation given above from
Polycarp).

2. Unless we admit the possibility of some
such free handling of the words, we shall have
to attribute each quotation to a different lost
Gospel.

3. These lost Gospels, if they existed, did
not, as far as proof can be obtained, differ
materially from ours.

4. The quotations may be by memory from
oral tradition, and not from any book at all.

The last conclusion is an important one.
There is nothing derogatory to our Gospels in
the supposition that men who had sat at the
feet of the apostles and other eye-witnesses of
the works of Christ would prefer, when they

could, to recall *their* words rather than to quote
from a book. Those who had seen the glowing
face or quivering lip of one who told how he
had *seen the Lord,* would find any written
narrative lifeless in comparison. To such men
the Gospels would be a Revised Version esteemed
more correct but loved far less than the familiar
Authorized Version; and such men the Apostolic
Fathers most probably were.

After all, it is not the form for its own sake
but the form for the sake of the substance about
which we inquire. Now, in the case of the
Apostolic Fathers, if we are doubtful about the
form, we are sure about the substance. We
cannot prove that the Apostolic Fathers used
any written Gospels at all, either our own
Gospels or lost ones; but there is no doubt that
the story of the Christ which they accepted is
the story given by our four evangelists.

" Christ, we read, our God, the Eternal Word,
the Lord and Creator of the World, who was
with the Father before time began, humbled
Himself, and came down from heaven, and was
manifested in the flesh, and was born of the
Virgin Mary, of the race of David according to
the flesh; and a star of exceeding brightness

appeared at His birth. Afterwards He was
baptized by John, *to fulfil all righteousness ;*
and then speaking His Father's message, He
invited not the righteous but sinners to come to
Him. Perfume was poured *over His head*—an
emblem of the immortality which He breathed
on the Church. At length, under Herod and
Pontius Pilate, He was crucified, and vinegar
and gall were offered Him to drink. But, on the
first day of the week, He rose from the dead, the
first-fruits of the grave ; and many prophets
were raised by Him for whom they had waited.
After His resurrection, He ate with His disciples,
and showed them that He was not an incorporeal
spirit. And He ascended into Heaven, and sat
down on the right hand of the Father, and thence
He shall come to judge the quick and the dead"
(Westcott, "Canon," 4th edit., p. 52, where the
detailed references to the Fathers are given).

Only one important feature will be missed.
There are no references in the Apostolic Fathers
to the miracles performed by our Lord. No
doubt, as Bishop Westcott says, all miracles are
implicitly included in the Incarnation and the
Resurrection ; but we must attribute the silence
of the Apostolic Fathers on the subject at least

M

in part to accident. No one of the Apostolic Fathers attempts to write a life of Christ; the details given by Bishop Westcott have been collected from all parts of their works. Moreover, it can be proved that Polycarp at least was acquainted with the miracles of the Lord. In the fragment of Irenæus's letter to Florinus, preserved by Eusebius (v. 20), we read as follows :—

" Whatsoever things he had heard from them (*i.e.* John and the rest who had seen the Lord) about the Lord and about His *mighty* works, and about His teaching, Polycarp, as having received them from eye-witnesses of the life of the Word, would relate altogether in accordance with the Scriptures."

A consideration of the whole of the foregoing evidence, gathered by working backwards from the opening of the third century to the close of the first, leads us to the conclusion that throughout the second century our Four Gospels were regarded as the chief authoritative documents of the Christian Faith. Yet this conclusion is resolutely rejected by some scholars of good name.

It is important, therefore, to realize the grounds on which the rejection is made.

These scholars refuse to accept the quotations of Justin as testimony to the existence or to the authority of our Gospels, because of difference of *wording.* Difference as to matters of fact is not alleged. The question at most is between our Gospels and Gospels which closely agreed with them.

In the case of Tatian, it is a question between our Gospels and an unknown Gospel or Gospels, which sufficiently resembled ours to be mistaken for extracts from them. With regard to the Elder quoted by Papias, it is a question between our S. Mark and a S. Mark which our S. Mark entirely superseded, presumably because there was sufficient likeness between the two writings to make an exchange possible.

In the extant works of the Fathers, from the close of the first century to the opening of the third, we find no trace whatever of Gospels substantially different from our own.

The evidence is fragmentary, but coming as it does with unanimity from many different sources, it is hardly to be resisted. *Either our Gospels, or Gospels which closely agreed with them.* There is no other choice.

That which has been said of the Apostolic

Fathers may be said with a difference of the great Epistles of S. Paul, which are generally allowed to have been written before 60 A.D. These Epistles cannot bear witness to the authority attributed to our Gospels, for the sufficient reason that our Gospels were probably written later. But these Epistles bear as strong testimony as the Apostolic Fathers to the story contained in the Gospels. We use as witnesses only the four following Epistles: Romans, 1 and 2 Corinthians, and Galatians, for the genuineness of each of the remaining Epistles of S. Paul has been hotly disputed at some time or other, and the testimony to be given must be beyond dispute.

Remembering, then, that the Epistles are not histories of Christ's life, we nevertheless find that by piecing together allusions contained in them, we get the following outline, which agrees no less with S. John than with the Synoptists :—

Christ Jesus was Son of God, but was descended from David "according to the flesh" (Rom.). He was sinless, meek and gentle, and He embraced a life of poverty (2 Cor.). He had a brother named James, who became in S. Paul's day a pillar of the Church at Jerusalem, "Kephas and John" being also pillars (Gal.). He did not come to abolish the law, but to fulfil it, for He is called a "Minister of Circumcision" (Rom.); but, on the other hand, His teaching brought freedom (Gal.). The key-note of His life was that "He pleased not Himself" (Rom.). He was betrayed to death, and on the night of His betrayal instituted the Lord's Supper as a memorial of Himself. He was crucified and was raised the third day, and was seen on several occasions after His Resurrection, and in particular by Kephas and by "The Twelve" (1 Cor.). Through Him God will judge the world, for He is the Mediator between God and man (Rom.); through Him all things were made (1 Cor.).

We have noticed no probable reference to the miracles worked by our Lord; but as a set-off to this, it must be remembered (*a*) that the Incarnation is assumed in these Epistles, and the Resurrection is mentioned over and over again; and (*b*) that S. Paul assumes, as an ordinary well-known fact, the exercise of powers of healing in the Church of his own day (1 Cor. xii. 9, 10).

CHAPTER VIII.

THE UNCANONICAL GOSPELS.

Gospels still extant—Their nature—Their witness to the
Canonical Four—Gospels known only from fragments—The
recently discovered "Gospel of Peter"—"The Gospel according to the Hebrews."

A FEW words must be said about these Gospels,
for anything which professes to be an original
life of our Lord is worthy of attention. They
may be divided into two classes: (1) Works
known to us only through fragments or brief
quotations, and (2) works preserved entire.
Something will be said in this place about each
class.

1. UNCANONICAL GOSPELS STILL EXTANT.

None of the Apocryphal writings still extant
are complete Gospels, even in the limited sense
in which our Four may be called complete. As

a matter of fact, they presuppose our Gospels
and enlarge on some part of the Canonical story.
Most of them are either Gospels of the Nativity,
or Gospels of the Passion.

Either class would serve our purpose of show-
ing the wide gulf separating them from the Four.
As it is hardly worth while to go at great length
into a description of these productions, we will
choose the Gospels of the Infancy. There are
three of these, which are to a large extent
parallel; they are Synoptics, so to speak, but
Synoptics with a difference. They are the
Gospels of Thomas, of Pseudo-Matthew, and the
Arabic Gospel.

The chief stories which the three narrate in
common are—

1. Jesus makes pools on the sabbath day, and
makes mud sparrows which fly at His command.
Annas, a priest (or a priest's son), destroys the
pools and is struck dead.

2. A boy is struck dead for running rudely
(*or* violently) up against Jesus.

3. Two schoolmasters in succession try to
teach Jesus His letters. He refuses to learn, and
strikes the second schoolmaster dead for striking Him.

4. A boy, Zeno, falls from a roof, and Jesus is suspected, not unnaturally, of having killed him. Jesus raises Zeno, who explains everything.

5. Jesus is sent to the well to fetch water. He breaks the pitcher, and carries home the water in His cloak.

6. Joseph, in the carpenter's shop, makes a length of wood too short. Jesus stretches it to the right length for him.

7. A viper bites His brother James. Jesus cures him, and curses the viper, which bursts asunder.

All these events occur before Jesus is twelve years old. Two of the Apocryphal Gospels finish with an account of Jesus *teaching* the Doctors in the Temple (not merely hearing and asking questions); yet the account is clearly based on S. Luke. These Gospels were intended only to supply the gap left by the Synoptic Gospels, and so far they witness to those Gospels.

Some of those strange stories of the Infancy are ancient. One manuscript containing them has been assigned to the fifth century (Tischendorf's Latin palimpsest of "Thomas"), and Origen (fl. circ. 230 A.D.) mentions this Gospel by name.

If they are ancient, our Gospels must be yet more ancient.

' But there is a greater distinction between the extant Apocryphal Gospels and our own. The latter are nothing if not memorials of a Person who impressed more by His character than by His miracles; the former are a string of purposeless wonders. No Apocryphal Gospel would have dared to write, "He could do no mighty work because of their unbelief." No Apocryphal Gospel would have reported the words, " Except ye see signs and wonders, ye will not believe." The Uncanonical writings are a string of miracles with hardly a touch of human character or of moral force from beginning to end. There are no gracious sayings to interrupt the dreary catalogue of miracles, no parables, no words of love, no touches of tenderness. Nothing like S. Matt. viii. 3, " I will, be thou clean;" ix. 22, "Be of good cheer, daughter, thy faith hath saved thee;" ix. 36, "He was moved with compassion for (the multitudes), because they were distressed and scattered;" x. 8, "Freely ye received, freely give;" xi. 5, "The poor have good tidings preached to them;" xi. 28, "Come unto Me all that labour;" xiv. 22, "He constrained

N

the disciples to enter into the boat while He sent the multitudes away ; " xv. 32, " I will not send them away fasting ; " xviii. 14, " It is not the will of your Father . . . that one of these little ones should perish."

The Uncanonical Gospels breathe another atmosphere. An insult, a doubt is punished at once by death ; Jesus is nothing but a wayward child omnipotent.

The great difference between our Gospels and others is this, that our Gospels are penetrated through and through with the reverence and love of eye-witnesses who had seen the loving Lord of Life, while the Apocryphal Gospels are dominated by a spirit of gaping curiosity which " never knew the sacred dead."

2. UNCANONICAL GOSPELS KNOWN ONLY FROM FRAGMENTS.

First among these stands the so-called " Gospel of Peter." * From this writing we have no certain quotation, though its name is mentioned once at the end of the second century, once in the third, and in the fourth century by Eusebius. From these notices, all that we can gather as to its contents

* See Appendix for a translation of the entire fragment.

is (1) that in it the " Brethren of the Lord " are described as the sons of Joseph by a former wife, and (2) that its language was regarded as Docetic in tendency, *i.e.* as favouring the views of those who held that Christ the Son of God only *seemed* to suffer on the cross, and that the body which hung there was either the body of Simon of Cyrene or else a mere phantom.

It is possible, but not probable, that the following quotation of Clement of Alexandria (fl. 200 A.D.) may be drawn from this Gospel :—

Peter says that the Lord said to the Apostles, *" If therefore any one of Israel be willing to repent so as to believe upon God through My Name, his sins shall be forgiven him. After twelve years, go ye forth into the world, lest any say, We did not hear."*

It is quite likely, on the other hand, that the quotation is drawn from a different work, " The Preaching of Peter," which Clement refers to by name two or three times.

The recently recovered fragment of the Petrine Gospel begins with a reference to Pilate's hand-washing at the trial of the Lord, and comes to an end when apparently about to describe the return of the disciples to their fishing, after the Resurrection. It contains very many details not given in the Canonical Gospels, but otherwise agrees so closely with them that it might reasonably be supposed to be written to supplement them. Its discovery in no way affects the position of the Four Gospels, except that upon the above supposition we have an additional argument for their great antiquity, for if this ancient work was written as a supplement, the works supplemented must be more ancient still.

It may be well, in this place, to call attention to the strength of the position occupied by the Gospel story, owing to the fact that we have four versions of it told at length. The Four Gospels are sufficiently unlike each other to be in a true sense independent works, so that their agreement carries us back to a source earlier than the earliest of them. The discovery of a new Gospel can hardly have an important effect on the position of the Gospel story. The new work will either agree with our present Gospels, in which case it will strengthen the position more or less, or it will disagree, in which case a single cord is pitted against a fourfold one. If, indeed, a new Gospel yet to be discovered can be proved to be earlier, not only than the earliest of our Four, but also than the early source, written or oral, to the existence of which our Four Gospels bear witness, then, and not till then, will a new and difficult problem as to the priority of the two narratives arise.

The following are characteristic instances of details given in the "Gospel of Peter," but not contained in any of our Four :—

The soldiers who mock Jesus seat Him on the Judgment-seat and cry, "Judge righteously, King of Israel." People go about with lamps, when darkness falls on the scene of the Crucifixion. The sun shines forth again after Jesus is "received up." The Jews are terrified, and exclaim that the Judgment and the Fall of Jerusalem are at hand. During the sabbath, a multitude goes forth from the city to see the sealed tomb. At the Resurrection, a voice from heaven asks, "Hast thou preached to them that sleep ?" (probably an allusion to Christ's preaching to the spirits in prison, 1 Pet. iii. 19). The disciples hide after the Crucifixion because the Jews wish to seize them on a charge of desiring to burn the Temple.

"THE GOSPEL ACCORDING TO THE HEBREWS."

A few words must be said about the Uncanonical Gospel best known in ancient times. This is not the Petrine Gospel, but "The Gospel according to the Hebrews," so called because it was written in Hebrew, and was used by Hebrew-speaking Christians. It is quoted by name by Clement of Alexandria (writing about 200 A.D.) at least once ("It is written in the Gospel according to Hebrews"); and apologetically by Origen (185–253 A.D.), with the formula, "If any pays heed to the Gospel according to Hebrews." Eusebius (writing about 324 A.D.) is uncertain whether to reckon this Gospel among the "Spurious." books, or to call it simply "Antilegomenon," *i.e.* "Disputed Book." Eusebius also gives the important information that Hegesippus (who wrote about 160–170 A.D.) made use of this Gospel It would be not unreasonable, on this evidence, to date the Gospel as early as 130–140 A.D. It may, of course, be still earlier. Zahn says that it was written more probably before 70 A.D. than after.

It is of very great importance to know something about a Gospel so well supported by ancient evidence; but, on the other hand, it is easy to overrate its importance. It is missing, and therefore missed. The one lost sheep, while lost, seems of more importance than the ninety and nine which went not astray. So, to a few writers, the "Gospel according to the Hebrews" has seemed to be worth more than all the Four Gospels we still possess.

But the "Hebrews" has not disappeared without leaving traces behind it, nor without making an apology for its disappearance. The fragments which remain, preserved chiefly by Jerome, show that it was a Gospel closely related to S. Matthew. Jerome at first thought that it was simply the Hebrew original of S. Matthew, of the existence of which Papias speaks, writing in 140–150 A.D. So, also, we find more than half the fragments (fifteen out of twenty-three) quoted as various readings or additions to the text of S. Matthew. The differences, however, are great enough to prove that neither work is a word for word translation of the other. Zahn's conclusion seems a true one, viz. that the "Hebrews" and S. Matthew are not independent in the sense and degree in which S. Mark and S. Luke are independent of the other Gospels. We should read only S. Matthew's story of the Christ if we possessed this greatest of the Apocryphal Gospels in its entirety. It disappeared in spite of the fact that Jerome translated it into Greek and Latin, because it contained nothing of importance which was not also contained in the Gospel according to S. Matthew.

Three instances in which the "Hebrews" adds something to the text of S. Matthew may be here given:—

1. In the account of the Temptation, our Lord is introduced, saying—

"*Just now My mother, the Holy Spirit, took Me by one of My hairs, and bore Me away to the great mountain Tabor.*"

S. Matthew simply says, "He was led up by the Spirit." With the expression, "My mother," applied to the Holy Spirit, compare the creed, "Conceived by the Holy Ghost." The metaphor is the same.

2. Eusebius says that this Gospel contained an account of a woman accused of many sins before the Lord (cf. S. John vii. 53; viii. 11).

3. Jerome preserves the following passage, which seems to refer to the appearance of our

Lord after His Resurrection mentioned by S.
Paul (1 Cor. xv. 7).

" But the Lord, when He had given the linen-
cloth to the servant of the priest, went to James
and appeared to him; for James had sworn
that he would not eat bread from that hour in
which he had drunk the cup of the Lord, until
he should see Him arising from them that sleep.
. . . Bring ye, saith the Lord, a table and bread.
. . . He took bread and blessed and brake and
gave to James the Just, and said, My brother,
eat thy bread, because the Son of Man has arisen
from them that sleep."

General Results.

1. It can be *proved* that after 180 A.D. all our
Four Gospels occupied the place of authorities
in the Churches *throughout the Christian world.*

2. Other Gospels, such as the "Gospel according to the Hebrews," and the " Gospel according
to the Egyptians," are quoted apologetically as
inferior authorities.

3. The Gospels publicly read in the churches
in the time of Justin, who wrote before 150 A.D.,
can be *proved* to be in substance identical with
our S. Matthew and S. Luke, and there are

o

indications that Justin knew S. Mark's and S. John's Gospels.

4. The authorship of our Gospel of S. Mark, and the fact that it contains a report of the testimony of S. Peter to the facts of our Lord's life, is attested by one who was, in all probability, himself a personal disciple of the Lord.

5. The Apostolic Fathers, whose testimony belongs to the period 96–118 A.D., in their brief Epistles still preserved, bear witness to the same Christian story as that contained in the Gospels —the pre-existence of Christ, His miraculous birth, His death and His resurrection, and the nature of His teaching.

6. The great Epistles of S. Paul, written before 60 A.D., give the same testimony.

7. So our Gospels contain no new story; indeed, the elements which have been most objected to are the oldest and the best attested. The Gospel story was a miraculous story from the first, though it was no mere miracle-chronicle, but the record how

"——The Word had breath, and wrought,
With human hands, the creed of creeds
In loveliness of perfect deeds,
More strong than all poetic thought."

CHAPTER IX.

A COLLECTION of these sayings is to be found in Bishop Westcott's "Introduction to the Gospels," Appendices C and D. A much larger number has been collected in a recent German work, Resch's "Agrapha." Yet the number of sayings really differing from the contents of our Gospels in *thought*, and attributed to our Lord in really early sources, is comparatively small. We will select a few of this small number, having regard to (1) the antiquity of the source, (2) their independence of anything contained in our Gospels. It is necessary to do this, because many so-called Apocryphal sayings are merely slightly varied versions of words recorded in one or other of the Four Gospels.

1. In the "Codex Bezæ," a manuscript of the Four Gospels and the Acts dating from the

sixth century, but certainly containing readings current as early as the second century, we read the following immediately after S. Luke vi. 4 (the incident of disciples rubbing corn with their hands on the sabbath day):—

"On the same day, seeing a certain man working on the sabbath, He said to him, *Man, if thou knowest what thou doest, blessed art thou; but if thou knowest not, thou art accursed and a transgressor of the law.*"

2. The great commentator Origen, the earliest of Biblical critics (185–253 A.D.), and several other writers, attribute to our Lord the following saying, "*Shew yourselves tried money-changers.*" These words are thus paraphrased in the Clementine Homilies, a work written perhaps in the second century, "*For it is thy part, O man, He saith, to try my words as silver is tried before money-changers.*"

3. Clement, Origen's predecessor as head of the Catechetical School of Alexandria, quotes from the lost "Gospel according to the Hebrews" the following, as a saying of the Lord: "*He that wonders shall reign; and he that reigns shall rest.*" We are reminded of our Lord's rebuke to the Pharisees recorded in the Canonical Gospels

for not considering the signs of the times. Only those who recognized by these signs the presence of the kingdom in their midst could share in the reign of the King.

4. Justin Martyr, a native of Samaria, who died probably about 150 A.D., writes thus : " Our Lord Jesus Christ said, *In whatsoever I find you, I will judge you.*"

Clement of Alexandria gives the same saying, with a slight change in the wording. The meaning seems to be that we shall be judged not only according to our deeds, but also according to our opportunities.

5. One of the most curious sayings attributed to our Lord has been preserved in the works of Irenæus (written about 190 A.D.), in a quotation probably from the lost work of Papias (written perhaps 140 A.D. It may have been much perverted in transmission. It runs as follows : " The Lord taught (of His future kingdom on earth), and said, '*The days will come in which vines will spring up, each having ten thousand stems, and on each stem ten thousand branches, and on each branch ten thousand shoots, and on each shoot ten thousand clusters, and on each cluster ten thousand grapes, and each grape*

when pressed shall yield five and twenty measures of wine. And when any saint shall have seized one cluster, another shall cry, I am a better cluster, take me; through me bless the Lord.' "

Bishop Westcott believes that this strange saying or parable is based upon some real discourse of our Lord; but at the same time he points out that it is preserved in a Latin translation of a quotation from Papias, who gave it on the authority of those who heard S. John speak of teaching of the Lord to such effect. In other words, it is the translation of the report of a report of a saying; and much importance must not be attributed to its details.

One or two other sayings might perhaps be considered sufficiently interesting to add to the foregoing list; but, in any case, this list must be a short one, for the good reason that the material available is very small in compass. The general results of a search for words of our Lord outside the limits of the Four Canonical Gospels cannot be pronounced to be successful. The English reader may, however, be reminded that two passages occurring in the English New Testament cannot be rightly regarded as parts of the

Gospels to which they are attached. The last twelve verses of the Gospel according to S. Mark and the story of the woman in adultery (S. John vii. 53—viii. 11) must strictly be regarded as very ancient documents containing weighty sayings of our Lord not known to us from the writings of the Four Evangelists. It was surely some special providence which preserved these two fragments " for our learning."

Neither the few sayings of our Lord recorded by others than the Four Evangelists, nor the fragments of Uncanonical Gospels, present or suggest to us any new story of the Life of Christ. The Four Gospels are in the most real sense of the word *complete*; they are the fullest revelation of the Christ which pen and ink can make.

APPENDIX.

TRANSLATION OF THE PETRINE FRAGMENT.

The "Gospel of Peter" is at present a fragment. We have but one manuscript of it, and that manuscript contains no more than would form about two ordinary chapters of the New Testament. It begins in the middle of a verse, and leaves off in the middle of a sentence. The title is, of course, lost, but we have no reason for doubting that the document to which this fragment belongs was known at the end of the second century as the "Gospel according to Peter." It reads as follows—

[According to Peter.]

"But of the Jews no one washed[1] his hands, nor indeed Herod, nor any of his judges, and of those who wished to wash. Pilate rose up, and then Herod the king commandeth the Lord to be taken, saying to them, Whatsoever I commanded you to do to Him, do ye.

[1] Matt. xxvii. 24.

P

" And there standeth there Joseph the friend of
Pilate and of the Lord, and knowing that they are
about to crucify Him, he came to Pilate, and asked for
the body of the Lord for burial. And Pilate sent to
Herod and asked His body, and Herod said, Brother
Pilate, unless some one had asked for Him, we would
have buried Him ourselves, since the sabbath is
dawning ; for it is written in the Law that the sun
set not on one put to death (*or* one murdered). And
he delivered Him to the people before the first day of
Unleavened Bread, their feast.

" And they took the Lord, and ran and pushed Him
and said, Let us drag the Son of God, now that we
have obtained power over Him. And they put on Him
a purple garment, and made Him sit on the judgment-
seat, saying, Judge righteously, King of Israel ! And
one of them brought a crown of thorns, and put it
upon the head of the Lord ; and others stood and spat
into His eyes, and others smote His cheeks. Others,
again, thrust at Him with a reed, and some scourged
Him, saying, With this honour we honour the Son
of God.

" And they brought two malefactors and crucified
the Lord between them ; but He kept silence as
having no pain. And when they had set up the cross,
they wrote upon it, This is the King of Israel. And
putting down His garments in His presence, they
divided them, and cast lots upon them. And a certain
one of those malefactors upbraided them, saying, *We*
suffer thus because of the evils which we did, but this

Man—when He became Saviour of men, what harm
did He unto you ? And they, being very wroth with
him, commanded that his legs should not be broken,
that he might die in torment.

"And it was midday, and darkness covered all
Judæa ; and they were troubled and in distress lest
the sun should have set while He yet lived ; for
it is written for them, That the sun set not on one
who has been put to death. And one of them said,
Give Him gall to drink with vinegar, and they
mixed it, and gave it to Him to drink. And they
fulfilled all things, and accomplished their sins upon
their head (*i.e.* against themselves). And many went
about with lamps, and thinking that it was night,
they were astonished.[2] And the Lord cried out, saying, My might, My might, thou hast forsaken Me ;
and when He had said it, He was taken up. And
that very hour the veil of the temple of Jerusalem
was broken in two. And then they drew out· the
nails from the hands of the Lord, and placed Him
upon the earth ; and all the earth quaked, and there
was great fear. Then the sun shone, and it was
found to be the ninth hour. And the Jews rejoiced,
and gave to Joseph His body, that he might bury it,
since he was a witness of whatsoever deeds of good
He did. And he, taking the Lord, washed Him and
rolled Him in linen, and brought Him into his own
tomb, called Joseph's Garden.

"Then the Jews and the elders and the priests,

[1] *i.e.* the malefactor.   [2] This word is uncertain.

knowing what evil they had done to themselves,
began to lament and say, Woe to our sins ; the judgment draweth nigh and the end of Jerusalem. But I,
with my companions, had sorrow, and being wounded
in mind, we hid ourselves ; for we were sought for
by them as malefactors and as desiring to burn the
temple. And, to add to all this, we were fasting, and
we sat mourning and weeping night and day until the
sabbath. And the scribes and Pharisees and elders
being gathered together, hearing that all the people
murmur and beat their breasts, saying, If through His
death, these so great signs are come to pass, behold,
He is righteous,—the elders feared and came to Pilate
beseeching him, and saying, Deliver to us soldiers, that
we may guard His tomb for three days, lest His disciples come and steal Him, and the people suppose
that He is risen from the dead, and do us harm. And
Pilate delivered to them Petronius the centurion, with
soldiers, to guard the sepulchre. And with them came
elders and scribes to the tomb, and all who were there
together rolled a great stone [1] against the centurion
and soldiers, and placed it at the door of the tomb ;
and they sealed it with seven seals, and they pitched
a tent there, and kept watch. And early, when the
sabbath was dawning, there came a multitude from
Jerusalem and the country round, that they might see
the tomb with the seals upon it.

 " And in the night on which the Lord's Day began

---

[1] These words are obscure ; perhaps they mean that the stone
was meant to exclude the guard.

to dawn, as the soldiers were keeping guard two and two, there was a great voice in heaven, and they saw the heavens opened and two men coming down from thence, having great light, and coming to the sepulchre. And that stone which had been put at the door rolled of itself and went aside; and the sepulchre was opened, and both young men entered in. Those soldiers, therefore, when they saw it, awakened from sleep the centurion and the elders, for they too were present keeping watch. And as they were declaring that which they had seen, they see again coming forth from the sepulchre three men, two of them supporting the third, and a cross following them. And the head of the two reached unto heaven, but the head of Him who was led by the hand by them was higher than the heavens. And they heard a voice out of heaven, saying, *Thou hast preached to them that sleep*, and a response was heard from the cross, *Yea*.[1]

"Those men therefore considered one with another to depart and inform Pilate of these things. And while they were still purposing this, the heavens again seem to be opened, and a certain man appeareth coming down and entering into the tomb. When the centurion and those who were with him saw these things by night, they hastened to Pilate, leaving the sepulchre which they were guarding, and declared all things which they had seen, being greatly distressed

[1] Or, *Thou hast preached to them that sleep, and by* [*Thy*] *obedience the Yea was heard from the cross.* (Cf. Phil. ii. 8, and 2 Cor. i. 19, 20, "In Him is the Yea.")

and saying, Truly He was Son of God. Pilate answered and said, *I* am pure from the blood of the Son of God, but ye decided on this deed. Then all came to him and besought him, and bade him command the centurion and the soldiers to tell nothing of the things which they had seen. For it is expedient for us, they say, to incur a very great sin before God, and not to fall into the hands of the people of the Jews and be stoned. Pilate therefore commanded the centurion and the soldiers to say nothing.

"And early on the Lord's Day, Mary Magdalene, the disciple [1] of the Lord (being afraid because of the Jews, since they were inflamed by wrath, she did not at the tomb of the Lord the things which women are wont to do over those who die and are beloved by them) taking with her the bowls [of spices] came to the tomb where He was laid. And they feared lest the Jews should see them, and said, If we were not able to weep and mourn on that day on which He was crucified, let us now do so at His tomb. But who shall roll away for us the stone which was laid at the door of the tomb, that we may enter in and sit beside Him, and do those things which we ought to do ? For the stone was great, and we fear lest some one see us. And if we cannot [enter in], even if [2] we put by the door that which we bring for a memorial of Him, we will weep and mourn until we come to our house.

"And when they had departed, they found the

---

[1] This word has the feminine form in the Greek.
[2] There is probably a corruption of the text here.

sepulchre opened ; and coming to it, they stooped in
there, and they see there a certain young man sitting
in the midst of the sepulchre, beautiful, and clothed
in a robe exceeding bright, who said to them, Why
come ye ? Whom seek ye ? Him, the Crucified ? He
is risen and gone away ; and if ye believe not, stoop
down and see the place where He lay that He is not
there ; for He is risen and gone away to that place
whence He was sent. Then the women fled affrighted.

"And it was the last day of Unleavened Bread, and
a good many were going forth [from the city], returning to their houses at the close of the feast. But
we, the twelve disciples of the Lord, were weeping
and sorrowing, and each one being grieved because of
that which was come to pass, departed to his house.
But I, Simon Peter, and Andrew my brother, taking
our nets, went away to the sea. And there was with
us Levi the son of Alphæus, whom the Lord . . ."

Here the fragment ends as abruptly as it began.
The text followed in the above translation is that of
Professor Swete, who has considerably improved the
text originally issued by M. U. Bouriant.

The following general conclusions suggest themselves on a careful study of the fragment :—

1. It is later than our Gospels.

2. It was composed in the main from our Gospels.

3. It contains a few particulars drawn from other
sources, perhaps from genuine traditions.

4. Its author was a Gnostic of the more moderate
type.

5. It is, like most Gnostic works, anti-Judaic in tone, *e.g.* it acquits Pilate, and lays all the blame of the Mocking and Crucifixion on the Jews and Herod.

6. It perverts the narrative of the Four Gospels in the interest of an anti-Judaic tendency.

7. It belongs probably to the second half of the second century, and is later than Tatian's "Diatessaron."

3/11/15

NOV 1915

PRINTED BY WILLIAM CLOWES AND SONS, LIMITED,
LONDON AND BECCLES.

CPSIA information can be obtained
at www.ICGtesting.com
Printed in the USA
BVHW040827010822
643515BV00002B/4